To Be a Pilgrim

The Life and Times of
Admiral Sir Alfred Phillipps Ryder KCB

They that go down to the sea in ships, that do business in great waters.

These see the works of the Lord, and his wonders in the deep.

Psalms 107:23-24

10 September 2019

Tony - with very
best wishes
Chris.

Chris Whitehead

Although the cover photograph of Hambleden was taken in June 2019, the view would have been instantly recognisable to the Ryders who lived there in the mid-nineteenth century. Their house, Hambleden Cottage, is the white building to the left of the rear cover. The old rectory, now a private house, is the prominent building to the right of the front cover. In between the Parish Church and the Manor House protrude among the trees.

Birch Cottage Publications
Pheasants' Hill
Hambleden
RG9 6SN

Email: chriswhitehead111@yahoo.com

ISBN 978-1-913218-43-0

Produced by Biddles Books Limited, King's Lynn, Norfolk

He who would valiant be 'gainst all disaster,
Let him in constancy follow the Master.
There's no discouragement shall make him once relent
His first avowed intent to be a pilgrim.

Who so beset him round with dismal stories
Do but themselves confound - his strength the more is.
No foes shall stay his might; though he with giants fight,
He will make good his right to be a pilgrim.

Since, Lord, Thou dost defend us with Thy Spirit,
We know we at the end, shall life inherit.
Then fancies flee away! I'll fear not what men say,
I'll labour night and day to be a pilgrim.

John Bunyan

Contents

Foreword

Some fifty years ago we inherited the letters and papers of Uncle Alfred, as he was known in the family. Among these were his beautifully illustrated letters of life in the Navy to his young son Eddy, written after the tragic death of his wife Louisa aged only 22. The letters gave me a little insight into life in the Royal Navy during the mid-Victorian period. What Chris Whitehead has done is to set Alfred's distinguished naval career in the context of the times in which he lived and served.

So in this very readable book we have the story of a generally little known Admiral of the Fleet in context. Chris presents the challenges of the Navy in peacetime which are otherwise only of interest to specialist historians: the evolution of steam power, screw propulsion, iron cladding and gun turrets. We learn of the establishment of lighthouses and issues to do with navigation and safety; education and the professional training of officers; also of Alfred's concern for the welfare of seamen, such as ventilation below decks, and their moral condition, reflecting his own evangelical piety.

Although knowing something of our family history I had not realised quite how significant the role that Hambleden played as the home base for Alfred when he returned from sea. I enjoyed reading of the Ryder family's relationships with the village and Church and with W H Smith and his family. The anecdotes to illustrate these, such as the Choir outing to London, bring Victorian Hambleden to life.

Beyond Hambleden we are given historical events and the cultural context of the times from the Crimean War to the American Civil War, from the Irish famine to the Opium Wars, the discoveries of science including Charles Darwin and the achievements of engineering. His father having been a Bishop, we read of Alfred's Christian faith and motivation. However, the story begins with and returns later to the circumstances of his drowning in the Thames, to which Chris gives thoughtful and sympathetic attention.

Like me, I hope you will find this book a way into understanding and feeling what life was like from the perspective of one man who lived through many changes and challenges during the mid-nineteenth century.

Lisle Ryder,
Alfred's great-great-nephew.
Yorkshire, July 2019

1

A Walk Beside the Thames

For this God is our God for ever and ever; he will be our guide
even to the end

Psalm 48:1

L ondon 1888.
Tuesday April 30th. 3.45 pm. The air is soft and balmy – a perfect Spring day.

Three elderly well-to-do gentlemen, all brothers, walk along the embankment to Vauxhall Pier from where they intend to take a steam boat to Battersea and enjoy a stroll round the park. One of the men is wearing the uniform and cap of a retired admiral.

Their conversation is wide ranging – how their sister Sophia's grandson, Edward, is doing so well as the youngest member of the House of Commons, even though he represents the Liberal Party; how, despite the impressive display by the Navy the previous year, when the fleet assembled at Spithead and was illuminated by coloured electric lighting at night as part of Queen Victoria's Golden Jubilee celebrations, there is some doubt about their ability to carry out coordinated exercises; about the gruesome murder only three weeks ago of Emma Elizabeth Smith, a prostitute in Whitechapel (they were not to know that five other women would be murdered over the course of the next three years by the hand of the infamous Jack the Ripper): a discussion about Mr Sullivan's new comic opera, The Mikado, that they had seen the previous evening at the Savoy Theatre, and how it bore no resemblance to the real Japan.

They buy their tickets, and two of them sit in the waiting room. The next boat is due in 15 minutes.

The third man, the one in uniform, paces up and down the jetty. As usual, he has a nervous speed to his step. Within minutes a cry goes up 'Man overboard!'. The two other brothers rush from the waiting room to see their brother struggling in the water some 60 yards away.

A captain of a tug throws him a lifebuoy, and a fisherman offers him an oar to cling to, but no attempt is made to grab either though they are only a yard from him.

The stream is running strongly at 4½ miles an hour and the drowning man is carried a full 100 yards before he is seen to throw up his arms and sink. It is all over in a minute.

The body is fished out of the river by the police some two hours later; because of the tides, it is from almost the exact spot it had entered the water.

The 'very sad and tragical' news of the drowning spreads through the begrimed streets of London 'with the greatest rapidity, and is received with sincere and heartfelt regret by the Admiralty' and a 'profound sensation' is felt in the lobby of the House of Commons – for the drowned man was Admiral Sir Alfred Ryder KCB, recently retired Admiral of the Fleet.

At the inquest one witness says that he saw him look to the right and left, step over one guard chain and under another, and then give a little run and jump into the water. Another witness corroborates this and says that it must have been a good jump or else the tide would have carried him against the timber of the pier. His doctor testifies that although the admiral was depressed and suffered from loss of memory and lack of sleep, he was not suicidal. He surmises that he must have suffered from an attack of giddiness that had caused him to fall into the water.

Perhaps to spare the family's feelings and the admiral's reputation – as taking your own life was illegal and widely viewed as shameful, suicides were denied a proper Christian burial - the inquest jury finds that 'the deceased dropped into the water while suffering from an epileptic fit'. No reference to epilepsy has been made during the inquest.

On May 5th his coffin of polished oak with brass furniture, is taken by train to Henley, and then by a funeral car of panelled glass drawn by four black horses, to Hambleden, where the Admiral was much loved. The funeral party arrives at 1.30. To the singing of the poignant hymn 140, he is buried behind the church next to his son, opposite the grave of his mother and sister, within sight of the old family home. Mourners include the Earl of Harrowby, five admirals including his close colleague Philip Colomb, the Chaplain of the Fleet, the Warden of St Thomas' Home Basingstoke, his brothers Richard and William and many, many villagers, but, tellingly, not his friend and erstwhile political superior, WH Smith.

The Rector wrote in the Parish Magazine….

> *The sad circumstances connected with Sir Alfred Ryder's death are so well known that it is quite unnecessary to repeat them. He was buried in Hambleden Churchyard on Saturday, May 5th, amidst many outward manifestations of loving respect. We offer to all his relatives our most sincere sympathy. The Ryder family has been connected with the Parish of Hambleden for so many years, and has been so universally respected, that in this time of sorrow it requires no effort on our part to make ourselves one with all the members of it in their trial. May God's blessing and comfort be theirs.*

This is his story.

2

Rule Britannia

Thou rulest the raging of the sea: when the waves thereof arise, thou stillest them.

Psalm 89:9

If there was any period in history when Britannia truly ruled the waves, it was in the sixty or so years following the final defeat of Napoleon in 1815. During this period, British sea power exercised a wider influence than has ever been seen in the history of maritime empires. The Royal Navy was virtually unchallengeable.

Its influence was not used to defeat traditional European rivals – they had already been crushed by 1815 in a long series of wars. Apart from a difficulty in the Crimea, the era was one of such unchallenged peace for Britain in Europe (though not elsewhere) that people came to refer to it as the 'Pax Britannica', and believed it would last forever.

For Britain, it heralded a period of free trade and of the creation of enormous wealth. To Britain, free trade was purely common sense – she depended on a growing world trade to take advantage of her great industrial lead, her large merchant marine and her financial expertise. She needed free trade to import cheap foreign goods – most importantly raw materials to fuel industrial expansion and foodstuffs to feed an increasingly urban population. The remarkable thing is that she was able to persuade other nations also to adopt free trade policies - at least to some extent – and to persuade them that they could absolutely rely on the Royal Navy to keep shipping lanes and ports open, free from pirates and privateers. Not unnaturally, many firms, individuals and states, in Europe and elsewhere, benefitted from these arrangements; the British did most of all. Today we would call free trade 'globalisation', which, as recent history has taught us, is a zero-sum game – there are winners and losers. The winners are those who lead in technology, are able to produce cheap natural resources and possess cheap labour. In the mid nineteenth century, this was Britain.

The political mantra was 'prosperity, progress and peace' which was to be achieved through the twin strategic and economic pillars of commerce and the colonies. The protection of Britain's ever-growing global trade was left to the Royal Navy. Britain's global reach as a naval and trading power was unrivalled. The Navy could close seas to its opponents and blockade their ports if it so chose. In these circumstances, no major power dared risk confrontation with Britain until 1914.

Despite peace and prosperity, the conventions and rituals of warfare were familiar parts of British life, and the memory of previous conflicts integral to the British psyche. Consequently, the battle fleet remained at all times in European waters to protect Britain from invasion and to intimidate her colonial rivals on their own doorsteps. With a small number of ships – and small ones at that – the Navy was able to encircle the globe. It was a power that did not have to be demonstrated very often - the emphasis was on influence rather than coercion; the mere presence of a nearby gunboat tended to exercise minds. The scarcity of naval actions is a measure of its success.

It meant that the Royal Navy was one of the greatest forces of deterrence the world has ever seen. It achieved an aura of invincibility – the pillar of national defence and the bedrock of the Empire. It's leaders, even in peacetime, were treated as minor royalty. They provided a source of entertainment, of sheer psychological gratification, to the population of Britain, who had an insatiable appetite for tales of military and naval derring-do in the far reaches of the world

Who were those men who led the Navy in the hundred or so years between Nelson and Fisher and Beatty, during this 'dark age' of modern British naval history; men who had to live with their golden predecessors breathing down their necks, but with neither their genius nor their opportunity? Miracles were expected; the 'Trafalgar Syndrome' was a lot to live up to, especially as Britain was at peace and the Navy's condition was considered of marginal interest by politicians. Governments were having to balance the need to protect trade and ensure the security of the British Isles with the ever-growing demands for budget restrictions.

Against this background, it is to its credit that, during the hundred years after Waterloo, the Navy transformed itself.

The accession of Queen Victoria to the throne in 1837 was the last occasion on which a new British monarch inherited a fleet made up almost entirely of ships built of wood and propelled by sails. In fact, it looked very much the same as in Nelson's day. The great ships were painted with alternate black and white instead of black and yellow bands around the hull, but were essentially the same bluff, oak-built sailing castles mounting cast cannon on elm carriages little changed from the time of Drake, manned and fought on the same principles exactly. In company and under sail they were magnificent. As instruments of policy of an island empire they had had no equal. A fleet of warships, to use Nelson's quip, were always the best negotiators. Or to quote Lord Palmerston *Diplomats and protocols are very good things, but there are no better peace-keepers than three-deckers.*

Magnificent they may have been, but redundant they had become. The Battle of Navarino in 1827 was the last to be fought by the Royal Navy entirely with sailing ships. By the Crimean War (1854-55) it was obvious to all that the future was one of steam and iron. By 1914 the fleet had changed to one of steam-driven, iron-hulled warships with guns in turrets - warships which would be recognisable to us today. Crews that had been press ganged, flogged and often inebriated were transformed to the professional, uniformed force we recognise in the twenty-first century.

Commerce, colonies, the Navy – an outstandingly strong framework for national and world power. Yet most of us would struggle to name just one of the admirals who directed the Navy during this dynamic period – a period in which the position of Britain was so pre-eminent that we are still living off its wealth to this day. We only remember (successful) fighting admirals, but during periods of peace another sort of officer is able to make his mark by laying the foundations for the next period of warfare. This was a period for intellectual naval officers who could set their minds to contemporary naval problems, be they matters of technology or welfare. Against a backdrop of unprecedented economic and technological change, a radical and far-reaching reassessment of the role of officers was required.

It was an age for officers with hungry minds, who were in a position to make things happen. They were as comfortable in their ability to represent the Queen in foreign courts as they were in maintaining the peace, in combating piracy, in avenging outrage, in preventing disorder among competing merchants and in captaining a warship – officers who were able to combine the role of diplomat and commander.

Such a man was Alfred Ryder, described in the Oxford Dictionary of National Biography as

> *A man of high attainments, who made persistent exertions to raise the standard of education in the navy. He devoted much of his time on shore to scientific study and was the author of some pamphlets on professional subjects, including one on a new method of determining distances at sea. A brilliant officer of considerable promise, he was a pioneer in the development of naval doctrine which was based on a combination of historical study and technical analysis.*

The following pages are about him, about how a Naval officer could make a name for himself in peacetime, and about the world in which he lived. It is also about the village of Hambleden in Buckinghamshire where the Ryder family lived for almost fifty years. Much of the village looks as it does today because of the family's generosity; after the WH Smiths, no family has contributed more to it. Yet they seem to have been airbrushed out of history, even though the Rector wrote in 1885 that *the honoured name of 'Ryder' is a household word in this Parish, and .... will never be forgotten.* He spoke too soon, for there is no mention of the family in AH Stanton's seminal work of 1927 on Hambleden *On Chiltern Slopes*, nor is Alfred Ryder mentioned in Margaret Verney's 1912 book *Bucks Biographies*, though there is a whole chapter dedicated to the sailors and soldiers of the county. Neither is his name found in many of the seminal works on the history of the Royal Navy.

This is the story of a devout Christian and a committed family man, two influences that would help him steer his course through the hierarchy of the Victorian Navy. His career may not have been 'exciting' in the traditional sense (though he did distinguish himself in conflict), but it was important, and it should not be forgotten.

I have referred to him as Alfred throughout, and to his friend WH Smith, as WHS.

3

Family Matters

Start children off on the way they should go, and even when
they are old, they will not turn from it.

Proverbs 22:6

Alfred Phillipps Ryder was born on 27th June 1820 in the Deanery in Wells, Somerset. He was baptised by his father, the Dean, just a few days later on 1st July.

Britain in 1820 was not a happy country – a land fit for heroes after Waterloo had failed to materialise. Peace brought neither prosperity nor plenty to a war-weary people. Triumph granted Britain dominance in international affairs, but it didn't feed people or give them jobs. As after every war, returning soldiers expected some form of recognition and acknowledgement. They found exactly the opposite – cuts in public spending, the cancellation of orders for additional military supplies and food prices kept artificially high by the Corn Laws. Together, they brought increasing hardship to many. No such fall in living standards and distrust in public institutions would be seen in Britain again until the 'austerity' period following the banking crisis of 2008.

A quarter of a million returning servicemen did nothing to help the economic slump that came with the end of wartime production. Work was scarce, especially in the North, where increasing industrialisation had replaced many traditional jobs. Moreover, cheap steam packet services between Dublin, Cork and Liverpool attracted tens of thousands of Irish immigrants, who were willing to take on gruelling work, often in harsh environments. Many of the dirtiest, least healthy and most dangerous jobs seemed to recruit a disproportionate number of Irish.

Who could the disaffected workers turn to for help? Trade Unions did not exist and most workers did not have the vote – so looking to their members of parliament was not an option. Presiding over it all was the bloated Prince Regent, who was as much reviled as the newly-restored Bourbon monarchy in France. In the same year as Waterloo, 'Prinny' had commissioned John Nash to turn his beach house in Brighton into a fantasy Moghul palace – the Royal Pavilion – and refurbish Carlton House at vast expense – much to the anxiety of the Cabinet.

Like the Trump-supporting interior of the United States in 2017 and the Brexit-supporting shires and northern industrial towns of Britain in 2016, disaffected workers felt ignored and left behind. As with these two groups, economic anxiety was not the whole story. Identity, immigration, nostalgia, a sense of reduced status, and alienation from the country taking shape around them all played their part as well. But, unlike those two twenty-first century groups, the workers of the 1810s had no electoral means to express themselves. Their only redress was on the streets, and demonstrations - against unemployment and high prices, against the monarchy and the constitution, and for the acquisition of political power - took place throughout the country between 1816 and 1819. The Spitalfields riot in December 1816 led in the following year to sharp measures for the suppression of 'seditious meetings' and the suspension of the Habeas Corpus Act. The government made little distinction between peaceful protesters and advocates of violent revolution. All unrest was dealt with severely; the hanging of ringleaders was not unusual in a climate where magistrates often failed to distinguish between agitators and sober reformers.

The impending storm finally broke at Manchester on 16 August 1819[1] when an estimated 60,000[2] men, women and children crowded on to St Peter's Field (now the site of the Radisson Hotel) to hear a powerful public speaker, Henry Hunt, call for representation in Parliament for the burgeoning industrialised towns of the Midlands and the North, who had no MPs in the Commons to speak up for their people.

The local magistrates, overlooking the Field from the windows of a nearby house, panicked when they saw the size of the crowd, read the

Riot Act and ordered Hunt to be arrested by special constables. Militia on horseback – including local publicans, some of whom were drunk – backed by the 15th Dragoons, who had fought at Waterloo, drew their sabres. The cavalry charged into the crowd lashing out with their swords indiscriminately. In the ensuing confusion, fifteen people were killed and many hundreds were injured. An eye witness later wrote[3]

> *Several mounds of human beings still remained where they had fallen, crushed down, and smothered. Some of these [were] still groaning … others, with staring eyes, were gasping for breath, and others would never breathe more … Persons might sometime be noticed peeping from attics and over the tall ridgings of houses, but they quickly withdrew, as if fearful of being observed, or unable to sustain the full gaze of a scene so hideous and abhorrent.*

A wonderful contemporary depiction of the scene, printed on a handkerchief, can be seen at https://www.bl.uk/collection-items/handkerchief-representing-the-peterloo-massacre

The massacre was given the name Peterloo in an ironic homage to a slightly more distinguished episode in these same soldiers' careers four years earlier. Peterloo was the first public meeting at which journalists from important, distant newspapers were present. John Edward Taylor, a local journalist, rushed a report on to the night coach to London, got it into the Times, and thus turned a Manchester demonstration into a national scandal. Taylor exposed the facts, without hysteria. By reporting what he had witnessed, he told the stories of the powerless, and held the powerful to account. Three years later he would start his own newspaper, the Manchester Guardian.

The impact of Peterloo was huge. The nation was horrified by the carnage; the historian, AJP Taylor, has said that Peterloo *began the breakup of the old order in England*. It remains a milestone in the long road to political reform which had begun with the egalitarian thinking that happened in and around the Civil War, and was to stretch by slow incremental changes until well into the twentieth century; it is arguably the most important political event ever to have taken place in Manchester.

Unrest was not eased by the succession of George IV in January 1820. The problem arose – what to do with his estranged wife, Caroline, whom he detested. He vowed she would never be the queen, and insisted on a divorce, which she refused. When she arrived back in England from her forced (but compensated) exile on 5 June, riots broke out in support of her. A constitutional crisis was on the cards, as Caroline was wildly popular with the British populace who regarded her as a figurehead for the growing Radical movement that demanded political reform and opposed the unpopular, obese king for his immoral behaviour. To women in particular she was a very public symbol of the repression felt by all. Not that Caroline was an angel – far from it; she was as morally wayward as her husband. Her licentious behaviour with her courtier, Bartolomeo Pergani, was infamous, as were allegations of semi-nude dancing at a ball in Geneva. It was said that in her room she had a clockwork Chinese figure that performed gross sexual movements when wound-up. Lord Norbury is said to have punned *She was as happy as the dey was long* of the relationship between Caroline and the Dey (governor) of Algiers.

The British public have always taken a lascivious interest in the breakdown of a royal marriage, and Caroline captured the imagination of the London mob who surrounded the House of Lords on every day that their lordships discussed allegations of her adultery, and escorted her coach with cheers whenever she had to appear there. Implausibly, she became the first 'People's Princess'. The public eagerly followed the scandalous revelations in parliament through the newly published twopenny broadsheets. Witnesses supporting the King's case presented evidence that the Queen had been seen in the arms of her Italian lover in various states of undress during her travels and that they had bathed together. One of Queen Caroline's Italian servants testified before the House of Lords that the Queen had employed a male exotic dancer, and proceeded to demonstrate aspects of the dance before the assembled peers.

George barred her from his coronation in July 1821. As one of the sixteen bishops of the Church of England, Henry Ryder, Bishop of Gloucester, Alfred's father, was present at the unseemly scene as she attempted to enter Westminster Abbey which was full of guests. A witness described how the Queen stood at the door fuming as bayonets were held under her chin until the Deputy Lord Chamberlain had the doors slammed in her face, and she was eventually persuaded to return to her carriage, the laughing stock of all those present. Opportunely for all concerned, apart from possibly the unfortunate Caroline herself, she died three weeks later. The whole affair was the talk of the country.

In February 1820, a month after the accession of the new king, hard economic times prompted a group of conspirators to exploit the political situation and attempt to murder the Prime Minister, Lord Liverpool, and several cabinet ministers while they dined at the house in Cato Street[4] of Alfred's uncle, Earl Harrowby, Lord President of the Council. However, the police had an informer and the plotters were captured. Five conspirators were transported to Australia and five were executed, quite gruesomely. The hanging took place at Newgate Prison in front of a crowd of many thousands, some having paid as much as three guineas for a good vantage point from the windows of houses overlooking the scaffold. After the bodies had hung for half an hour, they were lowered one at a time and an unidentified individual in a black mask decapitated them against an angled block with a small knife. Each beheading was accompanied by shouts, booing and hissing from the crowd and each head was displayed to the assembled spectators, being declared to be the head of a traitor, before being placed in a coffin with the remainder of the body. Public hangings were to continue in Britain until 1867.

Some historians have chosen these tense years between Waterloo and Peterloo to be the closest Britain had ever come to revolution since the 1640s, a period in which Earl Grey feared *a Jacobin Revolution more bloody than that of France*. Others maintain that the willing and able activity of the Lord Lieutenants, the Justices of the Peace, the militia, and the self-organised and self-ordered citizens of the towns, had sufficient resilience to keep order. The remarkable fact is, though, not that England of the Regency experienced considerable disorder, but that it did not experience a great deal more of it.

Percy Shelley summed the period up in his 1820 poem *England 1819*....

> *An old, mad, blind, despised, and dying King;*
> *Princes, the dregs of their dull race, who flow*
> *Through public scorn - mud from a muddy spring;*
> *Rulers who neither see nor feel nor know,*
> *But leechlike to their fainting country cling*
> *Till they drop, blind in blood, without a blow.*
> *A people starved and stabbed in th' untilled field;*
> *An army, whom liberticide and prey*
> *Makes as a two-edged sword to all who wield;*
> *Golden and sanguine laws which tempt and slay;*
> *Religion Christless, Godless—a book sealed;*
> *A senate, Time's worst statute, unrepealed—*
> *Are graves from which a glorious Phantom may*
> *Burst, to illumine our tempestuous day.*

So, in the middle of the Caroline crisis, in June 1820, Dean Close in Wells, overlooking the Green and the Cathedral, may not have been the scene of midsummer tranquillity that we might imagine – a tranquillity that was further disturbed by the hustle and bustle of servants and midwives as final arrangements were made for the baby who would be christened Alfred Phillipps Ryder.

Alfred was the seventh son of the Right Reverend Henry Dudley Ryder, Dean of Wells and Bishop of Gloucester, later to become the Bishop of Coventry and Lichfield. His mother was Sophia March-Phillipps, daughter of Thomas March-Phillipps, a wealthy landowner, a *most accomplished gentleman* and one-time High Sheriff of Leicestershire.

Bishop Henry was the third and youngest son of Nathaniel Ryder, the first Baron Harrowby of Sandon Hall in Staffordshire. The Baron had three sons – the eldest, Dudley, was Foreign Secretary and a confidant of William Pitt, the Younger. He was elevated to the peerage in 1809 with the grand title of Viscount Sandon, of Sandon in the County of Stafford, and Earl of Harrowby, in the County of Lincoln. He went on to serve as Lord President of the Council under Lord Liverpool; as we have seen, it was at a dinner at his house that the Cato Street conspirators intended to murder the Prime Minister and the Cabinet.

Richard, the middle brother, also went into politics, serving as Home Secretary under the fervent Evangelical, Spencer Perceval (who achieved a fame of sorts by becoming the only Prime Minister to be assassinated – by one John Bellingham in 1812). Incidentally, despite living nearly two hundred miles away, both brothers represented the rotten borough of Tiverton in Parliament, thus continuing the virtual monopoly of the Ryder family of at least one of the two seats allocated to that town for the ninety-nine years between 1733 and 1832.

With one brother inheriting the estate and the other forging a successful career in politics Henry was left with the army, the law or the church as a career. He chose the church. His first living was as a curate in the family parish of Sandon, and then to the parish of Lutterworth. His intellect and connections propelled him from being a country parson to a canonry at Windsor in 1808, with all the royal connections that that position entails. His sermons in St George's Chapel were said to be greatly admired by George III.

The Oxford Dictionary of National Biography describes Henry as a man of *literary taste, studious habits, and irreproachable conduct,* so it is not surprising that he went on to become successively (and in some cases simultaneously) the Dean of Wells (where Alfred was born), the Bishop of Gloucester, and, from 1824, Bishop of Lichfield and Coventry. You may imagine that growing up in this cloistered existence with servants aplenty, living in grand houses such as the Deanery at Wells and the seventeenth century Eccleshall Castle near Lichfield, must have been a tranquil childhood for young Alfred.

But you would be wrong! Any notion of uninterrupted peace within the precincts of churches and cathedrals would be a serious misconception. An overwhelming difference between the twenty-first century and the nineteenth was the presence of Christianity in society. It is difficult from a modern perspective to appreciate the importance of the Christian influence in the nineteenth century, not only on individual thought, but also on social convention and general attitudes. Religion mattered in a way that is incomprehensible to many people today. What you believed, what you didn't believe, mattered tremendously. It affected every area of life, public and private, social, political, educational, professional. Religion was arguably the most important mode of individual self-identity in nineteenth century Britain. The Church of England was the national church of the English people, the religious component of being English in the same way as were English citizenship and speaking the English language. Those who failed to conform were seen as disloyal, in particular Roman Catholics, who were seen to be in allegiance with England's traditional enemies, France and Spain.

In a world where death could come suddenly, and childbirth and infancy were dangerous periods in life, religion, with its promise of eternal life, was an ever-present solace. Clergymen enjoyed a greater prestige in society than they were later to do, and certainly more than they do today; their opinions were seen as important and carried social weight – they were respected, heeded and debated. But, on the other hand, the Church was seen to be part of the 'Old Corruption', mired in waste and extravagance in its higher echelons, and wielding sinister and unaccountable political influence.

By the 1810s there were widespread and well-justified fears that the Church of England was no longer engaging with the growing population in the rapidly expanding towns and cities in the industrialising north. Into this vacuum stepped various strains and strands of Nonconformity which offered a more engaged and plausible religion compared to that provided by what seemed the discredited and corrupt Anglican establishment. Nonetheless, the Evangelical movement that was closely associated with the abolition of the slave trade, demonstrated that there was still energy and commitment in the Church of England. Whereas High Churchmen believed that Scripture was the repository of divine knowledge and the purpose of worship was to proclaim respectability and to maintain the established social structure, by contrast, the Evangelicals were more concerned with conversion, faith and enthusiasm, although they too shared a commitment to law and order.

As a prominent member of the Church and a member of one of the leading families in the country, Henry was embroiled in the debate. During his early career at Windsor he was an adherent of the orthodox Church and viewed the Evangelicals with suspicion, but by the time he was translated to Gloucester, he had rather been persuaded by the intensely personal faith of the Evangelicals, expressed in strict standards of conduct and an inner conviction to spread the Gospel – a gentle, tolerant version of evangelism, concerned with improving the lot of the poor and improving access to education.

In 1815 a young John Keble was appointed curate of the beautiful St Michael and St Martin's Church, Eastleach Martin in Gloucestershire – a parish within Henry's Gloucester diocese. Twenty years later Keble was to become a prominent member of the Oxford Movement[5] – so prominent, in fact, that an Oxford college was named in his memory after his death. One can only imagine the discussions between the two men – two of the finest minds in the country. That such men should devote their intellect so completely to the service of Christianity suggests not only the important role that religion played in their era but the need they perceived for change and redefinition within the Church in line with the pervasive spirit of reform which was sweeping through society.

Henry's appointment to the Gloucester diocese was highly controversial. Because of their influence, the appointment of bishops was important; through their appointments Prime Ministers felt they could shape the character of the Church, and therefore the country, for decades to come, and so were driven by their own personal beliefs and preferences - not unlike the way American presidents are able to select members of the Supreme Court of the United States. When Henry was elevated to the diocese of Gloucester in 1815, he was the first Evangelical to be appointed to the Anglican episcopate – an appointment that may have owed much to the efforts of his brother, Earl Harrowby, then Lord President of the Council and an influential member of Lord Liverpool's administration. Liverpool's misgivings may have been eased by the particular form of

Henry's Evangelical doctrine – his attention to the poor and the sick and the diligence with which he undertook the Christian instruction of the young. His wisdom of avoiding a show of wealth and luxury fitted with the national preference for understatement.

Gloucester gave Henry his first taste of the problems associated with a mixed diocese. Although the county was mainly agricultural, during the eighteenth century, the city of Gloucester had developed into an industrial centre thanks to nearby deposits of iron ore, coal and timber from the Forest of Dean. Henry attempted to overcome the issues concerned with a lack of churches by actively promoting education – the introduction of day, evening, and Sunday schools for the particular benefit of the poor, and the establishment of the Gloucester Diocesan Society for the education of the poor.

In 1824 Henry was translated to Lichfield and Coventry, where he could deploy the same skills and vigour in another, larger, very mixed diocese, half of which was rapidly being transformed by urbanisation and industrialisation while the other half was somewhat bypassed by the industrial revolution.

Coventry was an example of the explosive development of an aggressively capitalist society – a unique and entirely unplanned experiment in profit-driven industrialisation. Nowhere else in the world had mankind ever had the opportunity to discover what would happen if you just left the rich to build lots of mills and factories packed with machines powered by coal and steam, and then set the poor to work in them.

By 1824 Coventry had grown from a city built on silk and ribbon weaving to become a major centre of a number of other clothing trades; nearly 10,000 workers were employed in the industry. It was also one of the three main centres of watch and clock manufacture in the country, with factories employing a number of specialised workers springing up alongside the workshops of individual master craftsmen. From 1825 to 1850 Coventry's business in watches almost doubled until it employed about 2,000 craftsmen.

During the first twenty years of the 19th century, people had flocked into the city attracted by the opportunities of working in the two main industries. They all had to be housed. Until the early nineteenth century most of the poorer inhabitants of the city were living in the ancient timber-framed houses in the less prosperous streets which had often been divided up, each bay of a building forming a separate tenement. The advance of modern methods of industrial production led to dwellings being rapidly erected in yards, gardens, and patches of open ground to house the growing population of ribbon-weavers and others. Many gardens were rapidly built up with parallel rows of small dwellings and back-to-backs, often with weavers' workshops on their upper floors. Passages through or between the houses on the street frontages provided the only access to these crowded and often insanitary courts.

These were the grim conditions in which many of Henry's parishioners lived. No amount of preaching from the pulpit of the medieval St Michael's church (later to become the cathedral that was destroyed by the Luftwaffe in 1940) was going to relieve it. In Coventry, as elsewhere in new industrial centres, clergymen had to fight hard to make the Church appear relevant in an increasingly materialistic and less deferential age. In such mushrooming communities, the provision of church space for the majority of the population was lamentably inadequate - there was church accommodation for scarcely one tenth of the population.

The government was aware that the established Church was becoming vulnerable to radical and non-conformist criticism, and so, contrary to the prevailing ideology of laissez-faire, agreed to grant a million pounds for *promoting public worship by obtaining additional church room for the middle and lower classes.* Today we see hundreds of urban churches built around this time – not least in Coventry. Here as elsewhere the new churches attracted new schools, so by 1830 the majority of children attended a school (possibly only Sunday School) for at least some part of their childhood, and most of the British population under the age of twenty was more or less literate.

Lichfield, on the other hand, was much smaller with a population of no more than 6,000, though it boasted a fabulous three-spired cathedral dating from the year 700. The city had flourished in the 18th century, and grew in national importance, becoming a centre of culture and learning. With the influence of Erasmus Darwin and his colleagues of the Lunar Society, Samuel Johnson and the great antiquarian, Elias Ashmole, Lichfield became a notable centre. Here was an interesting dynamic with religion and scientific advancement creatively interrelated alongside music, literature and culture, with Lichfield regarded as a major centre of enlightenment within Europe.

It also thrived as a busy coaching centre on the main routes from London to the north east, and to Birmingham and the north-west. Inns and hostelries grew up to provide accommodation, and industries dependent on the coaching trade such as coach builders, corn and hay merchants, saddlers and tanneries began to thrive. The main source of wealth to the city came from the money generated by its many visitors – wealth that was used in the early nineteenth century to rebuild much of the medieval city with the red-brick Georgian style buildings still to be seen today. Also during this time, the city's infrastructure underwent great improvements, with underground sewerage systems, paved streets and gas-powered street lighting.

A word here for Sophia, Bishop Henry's wife and the mother of thirteen children between 1803 and 1825. It was she who held the family together while the Bishop was working in the community or attending sittings in the House of Lords. When he died she had to give up living in the accommodation provided for the Bishop and find a new home for herself and the two children still at home – eleven-year old Spencer and fourteen-year old Richard. A home was found for them in Hambleden, a tiny, poor farming community situated at the foot of the Chilterns, between Henley on Thames and Marlow.

Getting from Lichfield to Hambleden today is not a journey to be taken lightly, even without two children in tow; imagine doing it in 1838! Firstly, a carriage to Coventry, and the train to London; stay a few days with daughter Anna and her husband Sir George Grey at their Eaton Place residence; then a carriage along the Bath Road to Twyford, and finally through Henley[6] to deepest, darkest Hambleden. There she was met by the Rector together with her own servants who had been sent on ahead to prepare the house. The house may have been prepared, but she could not have been ready for the way of life that awaited her. Although she was regarded as something akin to royalty (widow of a Bishop, mother in law of a member of the government), the village could not provide the mod-cons that she had been used to. For a start, she had to familiarise herself with the local accent.[7] The rector was the only other person in the village who could demonstrate any degree of literacy, so intelligent conversation was at a premium. How she must have missed her husband and longed for the life that was.

She must have been a robust woman – she bore thirteen children in an age in which it was not the practice to aid births by the use of instruments such as forceps. Childbirth was a risky business. In Hambleden, admittedly in much humbler circumstances than the Ryders experienced, one child in seven died before the age of five, one mother in twenty died in childbirth. One of the rites of the Church of England was the 'Churching of Women', the ceremony wherein a blessing was given to mothers after recovery from childbirth and as a thanksgiving for the birth of the child: *Forasmuch as it hath pleased Almighty God of his goodness to give you safe deliverance, and hath preserved you in the great danger of childbirth...* It has now fallen out of use, but the modern Baptism rite does include a prayer of deliverance. So, everybody knew about the risks involved, particularly those women who were about to go through the process, Death in relation to childbirth was mostly suffered by fit young women who had been quite well before becoming pregnant.

Such a person was Princess Charlotte, the daughter of the Prince of Wales, a young woman described as abounding in good health and brilliant high spirits. She had married Leopold, Prince of Saxe-Coburg in May 1816, and had become pregnant in January 1817 to much public rejoicing. During her pregnancy, she was advised:

> *to rise at nine o'clock every morning;*
> *to take breakfast before ten o'clock;*

> *to eat a little cold meat or some fruit and bread about two o'clock for lunch;*
>
> *to dine on food plainly cooked and easy to digest;*
>
> *to have no more than two glasses of wine at and after dinner;*
>
> *to take gentle exercise either on horseback or on foot every day that the weather was suitable;*
>
> *to take a shower every second day, the water being tepid at first;*
>
> *to have the loins sponged with cold water each day.*

In general, this is sound advice for a pregnant woman, and we may assume that Sophia followed a similar regime, although, by modern standards, the diet is perhaps less sustaining than is desirable – the importance of maintaining a sufficient quantity of iron in the diet from meat and vegetables was not appreciated at the time.

Despite having the best obstetricians in the country, Charlotte and her son died in a very painful childbirth – anaesthesia was not used in Britain until Queen Victoria made history in 1853 by becoming the first royal personage to give birth using chloroform. For the unfortunate Charlotte, the royal doctor, Sir Richard Croft, had relied on blood-letting to alleviate her labour pains and headaches – a practice that would have aggravated any anaemia present.[8] The country was stunned by the news of her death – it was as if every home in the country had lost a favourite child. There was a national sense of the deepest sorrow and disappointment – the golden prospect for the future had been dashed. Everyone, regardless of rank and station wore signs of mourning. Bishop Henry preached sermons to packed churches.

Incidentally, the death of Charlotte and her son had two significant effects on world history. Three months after Charlotte's death, and while attending another young woman who, with her infant, also catastrophically died giving birth, Sir Richard, still bereft with guilt, snatched up a gun and fatally shot himself. The unique triple obstetric tragedy - death of child, mother, and practitioner - led to significant changes in obstetric practice, with obstetricians who favoured intervention in protracted labour, including in particular more liberal use of forceps, gaining ground over those who did not.

But perhaps more importantly, if she had survived her father George IV who died in 1830, Charlotte would have become Queen of the United Kingdom, and her son in due course would have become King. There would have been no Queen Victoria – and the whole course of world history would have been different.

By the time of Charlotte's death, thirty-six-year-old Sophia and forty-year-old Henry already had eight children, and Sophia was four months pregnant with their ninth – surely a good enough family even by the standards of the day. So why, having been made so aware of the risks by such a high-profile case, did they proceed to have four more children? Was it something to do with the accepted view of male sexuality? It was an established truth, endorsed by the Church, that all men were possessed of a naturally strong sexual appetite, a characteristic admired by both sexes. A man without libido could not resolutely be called a 'man'. Sex with a woman was held to be the perfect cure for a range of male health problems, including fatigue and headaches – both of which Henry suffered from. So perhaps that was it – sex as a therapy, and a large family as the manifestation of Henry's virility. Or simply, Sophia and Henry just loved children and family life.

Henry grappled with maintaining a work-life balance. Nineteenth century bishops carried an enormous workload. As well as conducting services (a bishop's sermons were important as the touchstone of his ministry), managing the religious life of the cathedral and his parishes, he would write up to forty letters a day, oversee the building of new churches and schools, and attend sittings of the House of Lords. Today we understand how the cumulative effect of increased working hours can prove to be damaging to mental well-being; the more hours we spend at work, the more hours outside of work we are likely to spend thinking or worrying about it. This in turn can lead to physical and mental health problems, poor relationships and a poor home life.

In 1836 this is how Henry felt. Feeling ill through stress and overwork, he suffered a breakdown, and was persuaded to take a holiday on the south coast at Hastings in the hope that the sea air would invigorate him. Sadly, he failed to recover, died and was buried, far from his family and the home he loved. It says something for his ministry – the way he had placed social support for the needy above rhetoric – that a new church was built in his memory in a populous suburb of Birmingham. The Bishop Ryder Memorial Church was built on Gem Street in Gosta Green in 1838. The church was demolished in 1960 and Gem Street no longer exists – it was located in the middle of what is now the Aston University campus.

Henry's true legacy was his family. Their devoutness gave him and Sophia great satisfaction, even though they were divided by the Oxford Movement debate - two sons became Catholic priests and a daughter became a nun. Daily family prayers were the nexus of their life – the only time the whole family, including servants, got together. It was a practice that Sophia continued in Hambleden after Henry had died.

The influences on Alfred's early years were his parents; after the death of his father, he looked to Sir George Grey, who had married his sister Anna on August 14, 1827. Grey had been educated privately at Pyrton (a mile from Watlington) before going up to Oxford. He had intended to enter the church and had spent two years studying theology, but had abandoned that vocation for the law. He was described as *careful in action and moderate in speech, of tall and commanding figure, endued with genuine kindliness and genial manners, he was known to be a man of high character whose words could be implicitly trusted.*

Anna and Sir George were to live the next fifty-five years together, often in Hambleden in their early years – in the census of June 1841, Anna was recorded as residing at The Cottage - though their family home was the Fallodon estate, between Bamburgh and Alnwick, in Northumberland. Sir George became de facto the senior male in the Ryder family after the death of Bishop Henry and assumed responsibility for them notwith-standing his political responsibilities. He was, as he deserved to be, adored by them all.

The bond between Anna and Sir George was based on a devout Evangelicalism, inherited in both cases from their parents. Such was their faith that their political backgrounds were overlooked - the Greys were staunch Whigs and the Ryders staunch Tories. Two of Bishop Henry's elder brothers had been prominent members of Tory governments in the early nineteenth century, whereas Sir George was a member of a Whig dynasty. He was a nephew of Charles, 2nd Earl Grey, Prime Minister between 1830 and 1834, the man responsible for two history-changing pieces of legislation.

The first was the 1832 Reform Act, the culmination of popular agitations and political showdowns, when Earl Grey bowed to the will of the people and accepted the first step towards expanding democracy in Britain.

The 1830s had begun badly for the Government with numerous acts of arson, machine breaking and the sending of threatening letters. Popularly known as the 'Swing Riots', this series of disturbances engulfed parts of rural South and South East England in the second half of 1830. Prompted by a decline in the prices of agricultural produce and wages, the introduction of threshing machines and an influx of Irish labour, the rioters wished to restore their standard of living. Although most of the attacks took place in rural areas, some were aimed at industrial rather than agricultural targets. For example, in High Wycombe a large group of paper-makers assembled at Flackwell Heath armed with sledge hammers and crow-bars. *The rioters crossed to the farm of Mr. Lansdale, who had a thrashing machine which was shortly broken into pieces. They then proceeded to Mr. Plaistow's paper-mill, at Loudwater, which they completely destroyed.*[9] The riot was eventually quelled, but the direct consequence was that, on top of several hundred mill workers losing their jobs, the wage of an agricultural labourer dropped from nine shillings a week in 1830 to just six shillings a week in 1834.

The riots should be seen in the context of a government under pressure to extend political rights – a pressure resisted by the Tories, but who were outvoted in Parliament. This led to prime minister Wellington's resignation and the formation of a new administration under Earl Grey. He had little choice but to pass legislation to increase the numbers of people entitled to vote and to redistribute some seats from the poorly populated 'rotten boroughs' to the new urban centres such as Birmingham, Bradford and Manchester.

Though the Act appeared revolutionary at the time – the sixty-three-year-old Duke of Wellington, bastion of the Tory old guard, predicted that it would spell the end of civilisation as he knew it – it was in reality a grand sleight of hand. Yes, some rotten boroughs were popularly enfranchised, more constituencies were allocated to the new conurbations, and the franchise was enlarged to one in seven of adult males; but Grey had always intended that there would be no capitulation to the demands for universal suffrage nor annual parliaments. He had always intended that the old system should be preserved – the landed interest remained dominant[10] and the overwhelming majority of the population remained unenfranchised. Nonetheless, we can say that the 1832 Reform Act launched modern democracy in Britain; it provided the watershed moment when the sovereignty of the people was established in fact, if not in law.

Britain, unlike other countries in the western world, was to march toward universal suffrage through a peaceful series of parliamentary acts, culminating nearly a hundred years later in the Representation of the People (Equal Franchise) Act 1928, when all citizens over the age of 21 were given the right to vote, regardless of gender or property qualifications.

Curiously, the Bishop's nephew, Viscount Sandon, despite his political affiliations and although his family had represented the rotten borough of Tiverton for decades, served in a junior ministerial position under Earl Grey in 1830 and joined his brother, Bishop Henry, in supporting the Earl in the preliminary parliamentary battles to the Reform Act in the House of Lords where the legislation was more contentious - a demonstration of the association of the two families.

The second of Earl Grey's reforms was the abolition of slavery throughout the British Empire. By 1833 slavery in Britain and British involvement in the slave trade had already been outlawed, but not slavery itself. The Slavery Abolition Act had its third reading in the House of Commons on 26 July 1833, three days before William Wilberforce died.

It received the Royal Assent a month later, on 28 August, and came into force the following year, on 1 August 1834.

The Government took out one of the largest loans in history to finance the slave compensation package required by the 1833 Act. Nathan Mayer Rothschild and his brother-in-law Moses Montefiore agreed to lend the British government £15m, with the government adding an additional £5m later. The total sum represented 40% of the government's yearly income, equivalent to some £300bn today. The abolition of slavery was a very big deal! It was the first and only time in history that a slaveholding society voluntarily abolished slavery. By withdrawing from the slave trade and slavery and then by freeing the slaves, Britain was effectively handing over lucrative markets to its continental rivals. The result was the economic ruin of the British West Indies, the rise of Cuba as the world's principal slave importer and sugar producer, and higher costs to British consumers.

You might expect this so-called 'slave compensation' to have gone to the freed slaves to redress the injustices they suffered. Instead, the money went exclusively to the owners of slaves, who were being compensated for the loss of what had, until then, been considered their property.

Today, 1834 feels so long ago; so far away. But taxes paid by current British taxpayers have been used to pay off the loan; the payments only ended in 2015. Generations of Britons have been paying for a huge slave-owner compensation package from the 1830s; living British citizens have helped pay to end the slave trade.

The awards made by the Slave Compensation Commission might appear monstrous today, but most contemporaries did not share that opinion. The sanctity of property rights, whether relating to goods, slaves or serfs, underpinned the legal system in Britain and many European countries, while the principle of compensating estate owners for the loss of servile labour was already embedded in European practice. Within this context, it is not surprising that the British state was willing to sanction substantial compensation to slave-owners, who, incidentally, were not just the super-rich. Recent research by historians at University College London has shown the striking diversity of the people who received compensation, from widows in York to clergymen in the Midlands, attorneys in Durham to glass manufacturers in Bristol. It is true, though, that most of the money did end up in the pockets of the richest citizens who owned the greatest number of slaves. More than 50% of the total compensation money went to just 6% of the total number of claimants.

Slavery ended just as the British Empire began to expand, almost absent mindedly: around 10,000,000 square miles of territory and roughly 400 million people were added to the British Empire during the nineteenth century; in Africa alone twenty-nine countries were added as part of the Scramble for Africa. The juxtaposition of these two phenomena fed into British racial stereotyping – that the British were the master race with a God-given right to rule the world, and that those they conquered were their natural-born inferiors. Even though slaves were freed, the racist myths that justified slavery persisted. Whites, as well as many blacks, took it to be a simple matter of fact that blacks were less intelligent, more violent and sexually dissolute, lazier and less concerned about personal cleanliness than whites. Influenced by, but distorting beyond recognition, the work of Darwin, nineteenth-century pseudo-scientists ranked humanity into races; Anglo-Saxons were self-evidently on top, Africans at the bottom. It would be another hundred and thirty years before the country was to see the first legislation to address racial discrimination, and another fifty before the royal family, the very antithesis of diversity, welcomed into their ranks someone whose ethnic heritage is both black and African.

Social reform moves slowly, and memories still linger. To this day, students petition for the hall of residence at Liverpool University named after William Gladstone to be renamed because of his stance on slavery, and Oxford campaigners want Cecil Rhodes' statue to be removed from the front of Oriel College because of his association with white supremacy in South Africa.

(In this context, it is perhaps pertinent to reflect on the provision in Rhodes' will that funded the establishment of Rhodes Scholarships, widely considered to be one of the world's most prestigious scholarships and the inspiration for the creation of a great many other awards across the globe. Which only goes to show that things are not always black and white!)

Despite these two great political landmarks, Earl Grey is perhaps better known for being the inspiration behind the eponymous tea - a tea that was specially blended to suit the water at Howick Hall, the family seat in Northumberland, using bergamot in particular to offset the preponderance of limestone in the local water. Lady Grey used it to entertain in London as a political hostess, and it proved so popular that she was asked if it could be sold to others, which is how it came to be marketed as a brand.

He is also known because of his relationship with Georgiana Cavendish, Duchess of Devonshire, popularised recently in the film 'The Duchess', by whom he had a daughter to add to the sixteen legitimate children he had by his wife.

Sir George Grey entered Parliament in 1832 and soon made his mark – no doubt, having an uncle as Prime Minister didn't stand in his way! He served as Home Secretary three times between 1846 and 1866. He proved to be no push-over.

His reputation was much enhanced by his handling of what some believed to be a serious revolutionary challenge by the Chartists in 1848 – a working-class movement for political reform. The movement sprang from the working-class disillusionment at the Great Reform Act of 1832. The movement demanded universal male suffrage; constituencies of equal numbers; payment for MPs, so anyone could stand for Parliament, not just the rich; an end to the property-owning qualification for MPs; a secret ballot; and annual Parliaments.

More than 7,000 regular soldiers were brought into London when the Chartist National Convention announced its intention to make a mass procession to Parliament on 10 April 1848. The Duke of Wellington was enlisted less as an actual commander of operations than as an extremely useful piece of popular propaganda – it would do no harm to allow potential rebels to believe they would be fighting, if violence did break out, against the victor of Waterloo. As it turned out, perhaps fortuitously, he was not needed - the troops were kept out of sight, and the streets were left under the control of an astonishing number of 85,000 special constables, enrolled under Grey's orders. When the Chartist meeting on Kennington Common passed off peacefully Grey was given much of the credit for averting the danger and avoiding loss of life. He was especially commended for ensuring that the Royal Family had left London for the Isle of Wight some days previously.

The movement petered out, but Chartism did succeed in the end. Within twenty years there were major extensions to the franchise, and all the demands on the Charter were eventually realised, with the exception, thankfully, of annual general elections. The enormous achievements of the Chartists are now forgotten, but they were the civil rights movement of the United Kingdom – powerless protesters, reflecting public opinion, demanding democracy by peaceful means.

How they would have viewed the Brexit Parliamentary debacle of 2018-19, we may only surmise. They, like the rest of the world, would no doubt have watched with bewilderment, despair and exasperation as the world's oldest democracy, the leader of a former empire, winner of two world wars, was reduced to becoming a laughing stock. Was this what they had campaigned for? The astonishing display of incompetence — the defeated votes, the confused explanations, the constant uncertainty — severely undermined the respect that people had for politics, for politicians, and for Parliament in general. And they would have been outraged when, in defiance of the principles of democratic representation, a cohort of 160,000 people, much richer, older and whiter than the general population, should impose their choice for Prime Minister on the rest. A modern rotten borough!

In the mid eighteen-hundreds, as today, the Home Secretary was responsible for penal policy. Following the abolition in 1853 of transportation for convicts, prisons expanded to accommodate the increased population of prisoners. Grey was a firm believer in the 'separate' system of prison discipline, convinced that the separation of convicts from one another, accompanied by religious instruction, would promote their moral reformation. He saw the criminal as a sinner, and regarded it as the task of the state to reform his or her character on an individual basis – paradoxically by promoting religious instruction and by providing for a harsh system of prison labour in local prisons.

He was convinced that capital punishment, on which he set up a royal commission in 1864, was a strong deterrent to deliberate murder, and was unwilling to exercise the prerogative of mercy. Although many among the onlookers at public executions were more or less inebriated before the proceedings – a recipe for rowdiness, pick pocketing and general bad behaviour – he felt that public hangings were useful exercises and not undermining of morals. He argued that large crowds of lower-class people always behaved disgustingly, be they at a hanging or any other spectacle. He maintained that public hangings were a good deterrent for....

> *who can tell in how many instances a deep and lasting impression may be made upon the minds even of some of the most criminal class, which may check them in a career of crime, and, inducing them to abstain from the course to which they are prompted by passion, vicious habits and early association, tend to rescue them from the same ignominious end?*

Sir George retired from public life to his Northumberland estate, and died there in 1882. Anna then moved to Alfred's house in Torquay, a town then popular amongst the rich and privileged of Europe. They lived there together, two aristocratic, possibly slightly eccentric elderly people - she being 77 and he 62 – until Alfred's death in 1888. She continued to live there with other elderly relatives till passing away in 1893 at the grand old age of 88.

George and Anna's grandson, Sir Edward Grey, had entered Parliament in 1885 and, at 23, became the youngest MP in the House of Commons. He was an excellent tennis player winning the British championship in 1889, 1891, 1895, 1896 and 1898, and being runner-up in 1892, 1893 and 1894, all years in which he was making a name for himself in the Commons. He was also a lifelong fly fisherman, publishing a book on his exploits in 1899, which remains one of the most popular books ever written on the subject

He was Foreign Secretary between 1906 and 1916, during one of the most traumatic periods of the country's history. After Germany had invaded Belgium on August 3, 1914, as he stood at a window in the Foreign Office watching the lamps being lit as dusk approached, Sir Edward is famously said to have remarked to the editor of the Westminster Gazette, *The lamps are going out all over Europe. We shall not see them lit again in our time.*

In 1919 Sir Edward, now Viscount Grey of Fallodon, was appointed Ambassador to the United States, a post he held until 1920. On his return, and with failing eyesight, he continued to be active in politics, serving as Leader of the Liberal Party in the House of Lords from 1923 until his resignation on the grounds that he was unable to attend on a regular basis in 1924.

The Grey family's association with Hambleden, however, is more than just through the Ryders. General Sir Charles Grey, one of the 2nd Earl's sixteen legitimate children represented Wycombe in the British House of Commons for the Whigs between 1832 and 1837, defeating Disraeli in the 1832 General Election – no mean feat – and it could be through that connection that Sophia moved to Hambleden in 1838 after the death of her husband. General Grey later obtained the influential positions of secretary to Prince Albert from 1849 to 1861, and secretary to the Queen from 1861 until his death in 1870. Another of the sixteen, Admiral the Hon. George Grey lived at Yewden Manor (a mile from Hambleden) between 1863 and 1874, and the Parish Magazine records his regular contributions towards the staff and running costs of Hambleden School.

So, although a widow for some twenty-six years, Sophia had been surrounded by her family for all of that time and The Cottage in Hambleden became their family home. When she died in 1862, the family had grown to twenty-four grandchildren, one of whom, Una, was born in The Cottage to her grandmother's delight. She also had four great grandchildren. She is buried in Hambleden Churchyard, at the west end of the church, in a grave designed by Alfred.

The Ryders continued to live in The Cottage until the death of Amelia, Sophia's second daughter, in 1885. The family had been resident in the village for forty-seven years; only the WH Smith family have donated more to the community. They were part of the village, and the village was part of them.

4

The Navy

Be strong and of a good courage; be not afraid, neither be thou dismayed: for the Lord thy God is with thee whithersoever thou goest.

Joshua 1:9

On November 4th 1805, two weeks after Trafalgar, the details of the death of Lord Nelson and his victory arrived in London. Within a week the news had spread through the kingdom. The admiral's final words 'Thank God I have done my duty' resonated with the country then as they still do to this day. Britain's greatest naval commander had died just as the last shots of the battle were being fired in the greatest naval victory his country had ever known or would ever know.

A battered *HMS Victory*, with Nelson's body on board reached Greenwich on Christmas Eve. His body was laid in the Painted Hall for a few days before the funeral at St Pauls, too damaged for the public to be permitted to see it in an open coffin. On January 8, a crowd of 30,000 had gathered to watch as his coffin was taken from Greenwich, transferred to a royal barge, and rowed to Westminster where it was to remain overnight in the Admiralty before being transferred to St Pauls. The weather next day was unusually fine for January. Huge crowds lined the route; the funeral column was so long that the Royal Scots Greys at the front had reached the cathedral before Nelson's remains had left the Admiralty. The crowds fell silent as the coffin approached, the only sound a noise like a murmur of waves along the seashore as thousands removed their hats in respect.[11]

Nelson's coffin was borne into St Pauls by eight admirals, all weeping. The funeral service was emotional and moving; the choir finished their solemn anthems by bursting into full cry with the line 'But his name liveth evermore'. After the words had died away, Nelson's coffin slowly disappeared, vanishing dramatically through a trapdoor into the crypt below. The whole congregation joined the pall bearers in their teary mourning.

With this story, Bishop Henry had young Alfred spellbound; to think that his father had been present in the cathedral and had witnessed the final proceedings of this truly national hero[12]. As we shall see, when the Hambleden choir visited London in July 1874, *they paid their respects to Nelson's coat and sword.* To this day, on 21 October each year the commissioned officers of the Royal Navy celebrate the victory at the Battle of Trafalgar by holding a Trafalgar Night dinner in the officer's mess and sea cadets hold a national parade in Trafalgar Square. Nelson's naval exploits were something that every young naval officer, indeed every young boy, in the early nineteenth century would seek to emulate; they weren't to know that Britain was about to enter a period of prolonged relative peace – the so-called Pax Britannica.

Just as we in Britain were suspicious of the Germans and the Japanese for decades after 1945, so Britain after Waterloo remained suspicious of the French. In fact, it is difficult for us to overestimate the extent of this paranoia. England and France had been hereditary enemies for much of the preceding half-millennium, but the Napoleonic Wars had dwarfed all earlier conflicts in terms of length, intensity and expense. Citizens of the time could not have known that the two nations would never again go to war against each other and would invariably be on the same side in future conflicts. But in 1833, not only did all the British military, and many of their politicians, continue to believe that the greatest political threat came from France (up to and even during the Crimean War when the French and the British were supposed to be allies), but they also believed that the prospect of a French invasion was possible, even after the possibility of such an event had been extinguished. Above all they saw France as the very object lesson of what could happen if a society imploded, and the only thing that stood between Britain and a resurgent France was the Navy. And furthermore, France was Catholic; memories of the middle ages still lingered - Catholics were prohibited from sitting in the Commons until 1829.

At the time, in the 1830s, as Alfred's parents were deliberating over his career, their views were swayed by Palmerston's foreign policy, which was to maintain the balance of power in Europe by keeping post-Napoleonic France in check and curbing Russia's expansionist ambitions towards India in the eastern Mediterranean and Asia. It was vital to protect and extend the opportunities for British traders and investors overseas by consolidating and expanding the United Kingdom's recently established position as the world's pre-eminent fiscal, industrial and trading power. Palmerston claimed in 1832 that *there never was a period when England was more respected than at present in her foreign relations, in consequence of her good faith, moderation and firmness.* The Royal Navy was the instrument of this policy and serving in it was a patriotic thing to do.

It was also a Christian thing to do. In 1808, the Royal Navy established the West Africa Squadron to suppress the Atlantic slave trade by patrolling the coast of West Africa – a cause perceived by Bishop Henry as part of the Evangelical mission. Abolitionists maintained that slavery was a violation of God's will. Since every human being possessed a soul, they argued that no human being could be made into another man's possession without also perverting the divine plan.

For centuries the Navy had protected the country's slave trade. Sugar, tobacco and cotton were the foundations of fabulous wealth and the fuel of industrialisation; slave labour was the engine of these industries. Nonetheless, from about 1787 William Wilberforce and other Evangelicals became horrified by what they perceived was a depraved and un-Christian trade, and of the greed and avarice of the owners and traders. They began to campaign against it – a campaign that resulted in the Abolition of the Slave Trade Act 1807, which, although not abolishing *slavery* itself, did abolish the *slave trade* in the British Empire. The abolition of slavery itself would take another twenty-six years, during which time Evangelicals naturally rejoiced when Bishop Henry became Bishop of Gloucester, the first bishop to be chosen from among their ranks, and one who would be able to lend support in the House of Lords. Wilberforce regarded him highly as *a prelate after his own heart, who united to the zeal of an apostle the most amiable and endearing qualities, and the polished manners of the best society.*

William Wilberforce's papers contain correspondence with the Bishop, his brother Dudley Ryder, (1st Earl of Harrowby), and George Ryder, Alfred's brother. George would, in fact, become linked, albeit tenuously, to the Wilberforce family when he married Sophia Sargent in 1834 the sister of two of Wilberforce's daughters in law.

Both the 1807 and 1832 Acts were steered through Parliament by Earl Grey. During the passage of the 1832 Act he was supported by his nephew Sir George Grey – Alfred's brother-in-law. The Ryders and Greys were thus closely associated with the suppression of slavery, and the possibility of becoming part of the crusade through the Royal Navy would have seemed an honourable career to pursue to the young Alfred. Not only was it honourable and Christian – the campaign against slavery was one of the most glorious in the Navy's history, and one of the few instances of a nation acting against its own interests to snuff out a manifest evil - but in the post-Trafalgar peace, it also promised excitement. Although an unrewarding, tedious, unhealthy and strenuous task, the West African Squadron was the training ground for a new generation of officers. Young captains learned the arts of hunting and pursuing an enemy, and developed the cunning and patience, the independence and resourcefulness of their great predecessors. Their vessels had to be small, swift and lightly armed – two-masted schooners, brigs and brigantines. The exploits of the brigs Black Jake and Buzzard[13] were pored over by the British public; their officers and men had to board larger enemy ships, cutlasses and pistols in hand, as their forebears had done in the classical age of sailing warfare. As it turned out, fighting slavers would barely feature at all in Alfred's career!

To add fuel to an already burning flame, young Alfred was enthralled by the early novels of Frederick Marryat - a retired naval officer who virtually founded naval fiction and became the most popular author of his day. His novels were based on his own experiences as a midshipman during the Napoleonic Wars and served to keep the service in the public eye with stories of fearless action and adventure. CS Forester and his hero Horatio Hornblower would captivate more boys a hundred years later, as would Patrick O'Brian's Aubrey–Maturin series another thirty years on.

One or two other factors enhanced the reputation of the Navy.

It was significant that when Napoleon surrendered for the final time, on 15 July 1815, it was to a naval captain on board *HMS Bellerophon*. 'What I admire most in your ship', he told the captain, 'is the extreme silence and orderly conduct of your men; on board a French ship everyone calls and gives orders, and they gabble like so many geese.' The same clockwork routine and unquestioning obedience to orders with which British sailors went about their daily shipboard tasks allowed them to fire their broadsides again and again in the heat of bloody, frenzied battles with withering regularity. They held a rather special place in the eyes of the British public - sort of amiable Crocodile Dundee figures. Jolly Jack Tar was fearless and competent in his own element where he braved the storms, defeated the country's enemies and stamped order into chaos; but on shore he was generous and slightly wild. His capacity for drink was legendary, and when he applied the rules of the sea to the land, be brought chaos into order! And of course, King William, who ruled from 1830 to 1837 – exactly the period during which Alfred's career would be decided – revived royal interest in the Navy. He had served under Nelson in 1780 and was dubbed the 'sailor king'.

Naval officers were seen as the epitome of a certain kind of Britishness. As with so many aspects of the national character, it was shot through with class – naval officers of the nineteenth century were a superior, even haughty bunch, and were members of one of the only five acknowledged professions, the others being the church, the law, medicine and the army. Drawn from the gentry and upper classes they may have been, but this did not distract from the high professional standards that the service insisted on. Aristocratic insouciance coexisted with uncompromising self-discipline and the clockwork routine long established in British warships. It was an odd mix of values: upper class yet methodical; urbane but technically competent; individualistic and collegiate at the same time. Like their crew, naval officers became entwined with the sense of national identity. They retained the expectation of victory bequeathed them by their predecessors. The image of a ship's company fighting alone far from home with limited resources, relying on their teamwork and ingenuity is a powerful one. It idealised a standard of masculinity and conduct; its sheer dominance and defiance made the Navy central to the British way of life – so much so that in the first months of the Great War every detail of the activities of the Royal Navy excited the British public more than anything their soldiers did, though the sailors' role was much less immediately significant. The British people continued to nurse a persistent delusion that the Royal Navy would fight a great battle against the Germans because this was what their heritage demanded - in defiance of the simple logic that the Germans, by dint of sheer weight of numbers, were unlikely to accept an engagement they could not expect to win.

Although to be a naval officer became fashionable and socially acceptable, it was perhaps not the obvious choice for a rather studious, deeply religious, boy. One may have thought that a more suitable career for Alfred might have been to follow his father into Holy Orders, as his brothers Henry and George had done. Sister Sophia had become a nun. Or perhaps the law, as elder brother William had done, and as younger brother Richard was to do. However, joining the Navy was not without precedent in the family. Charles, the Bishop's second son, had joined the Navy as a midshipman in 1820, but had drowned when a boat from *HMS Naiad* capsized in the mouth of the river Tiber in 1825.[14] He had been just eighteen years old; Alfred, not yet five, had barely known him.

However, joining the post-Napoleonic Navy was not without risks, for it was greatly diminished as the Government attempted to balance budgets after the long wars. The fleet was reduced from 1,009 ships in 1813 to 179 in 1826, only a few of which were in commission. Many of the old, great warships were decommissioned and broken up; others were laid up 'In Ordinary' for many years with no masts and rigging, no guns, and no maintenance crews. A considerable number of these ships had been launched and placed straight into Ordinary without ever being commissioned. The naval bases in the Medway, at Portsmouth, and at Plymouth were full of such vessels. Hulks were employed on duties such as depots, barracks and hospitals, and had no further wartime role. Not only was the Navy reduced, but it was also redistributed. Instead of consisting chiefly of fleets of ships of the line concentrated in home waters, the Baltic and the Mediterranean (where any real threat had been eliminated), it now had its energies and manpower diverted across the world – West Africa, the Cape, the East Indies and China, South America, the Pacific, the West Indies – to supress slavery and piracy and to protect British commercial interests

Manpower was cut just as dramatically – from 140,000 in 1815 to 23,000 in 1826. On being paid off, the sailors were simply landed on shore to make their way as best they could. The officers, however, continued to serve, but only a few were serving at sea and there were fifty competing for each appointment. Most officers who had begun their careers in the boom years found themselves ashore, on half pay, with little prospect of employment and even less of prize money. Advancement meant literally waiting for dead man's shoes. Not a career with promising prospects!

Unless, of course, the aspirant officer was fortunate enough to have 'interest' – political and family connections – which, as we have seen, Alfred had in abundance. However, even with good connections, as with Alfred's elder brother Charles, the traditional entry for hopeful volunteers (all of whom were in their very early teens) was to spend their first two years acquiring sailors' skills by working alongside the men on deck and aloft. Fundamentals of education were supplied by a Warrant Officer, as and when time permitted. Most boys, and captains, couldn't see the need for it. After two years the volunteer would expect to become a Midshipman and would serve in this capacity for another four years. However, such was the bottleneck of Lieutenants caused by the run down in the active fleet after the wars that he would not necessarily, or even probably, obtain a commission for several years after that – and many never did. The Midshipmen lived and messed in a dark and barely ventilated room below the waterline. Despite his connections, Jackie Fisher, later to become a respected reforming admiral, had joined the Navy this way in 1854. Later he reminisced….

We never washed because if you spilt a drop of water by your sea chest in which was a basin holding a pint of water, you had to dry holystone the deck, a holystone being a bath brick, and you rubbed the sand into the deck until the wood was spotless white. When the first bathroom was introduced into one of Her majesty's ships, I heard the First Sea Lord myself say to the Second Sea Lord 'Did you ever wash when you went to sea?' 'No' he replied. 'No more did I', said the First Lord.

Bullying was rife but was accepted as a way of weeding out the weak, the too-sensitive and others not suited to the rigours of sea life. But by developing an understanding how boats and sailors worked under all conditions, it made Midshipmen into superb seamen. It also tended to make them narrow minded, intolerant, insensitive, pig-headed, foul-mouthed and tyrannical; to be oversensitive and too collegiate would not have suited the conditions, nor would it have been respected by the men. The wonder is that so many survived without showing these traits.

Twenty years later, as a captain, Alfred rather viewed the young midshipmen on his own vessels as members of his family. He would refer to them as 'his boys' in the way one may expect from a Victorian father – kindly but distant. He described various incidents in letters to his son….

Papa had such a walk at Messina. He took a part of his big little boys on shore and walked them up to the top of a high hill, and then ran all the way down to the bottom.[15]

We went to a beautiful place called Palermo. Papa took some of his big boys into the country to see such a beautiful church – of which the ceiling looked like gold. It was all made of little pieces of glass. There was a very kind monk who showed Papa and his boys over the Church.[16]

Papa took it into his head the other day to take a good long walk. So he took two of his little boys, and good Mr Jacob the Chaplain and Ruby (the dog), and set off. But there are no nice fields in Malta, nothing but dusty roads. Papa and Mr Jacob walked so quick that the poor little boys had to run behind nearly the whole way. It was quite dark when we got back to the ship and the little boys were quite tired and had such a capital appetite. Papa gave them a good dinner.[17]

One of Papa's middies, not a very big boy, has been sick for six weeks with rheumatism – all his ankles and elbows and wrists and knees swelled up quite large, and he was in such pain. Papa sent him ashore to a large house called a hospital, where they took great care of him and now he is well again.[18]

I did punish a little middy last night. He was such a naughty little middy. It was not only what he did, but the excuse he made which almost made me laugh when I wanted to look very solemn and rather angry. You know that the middies have a Schoolmaster. He has 18 boys to teach. He and I have to keep them all in order. We are not allowed to whip them, but we manage to keep their heads the right way. The Schoolmaster came on deck and said 'If you please Captain Ryder, Mr K has been making my coat tails fast to the chair, so that when I got up I dragged the chair after me and all the other young gentleman began to laugh.' So I sent for young K, and asked him how he could think of doing such a saucy naughty thing, and what do you think his excuse was? 'Why', he said, 'the string was such a very little piece of string', as if it made any difference whether the string was short or long. So as a punishment, I made him stay up very late walking the deck, and get up gain very early and walk the deck again. You may think walking the deck is great fun, but little middies get very tired of it. And I think the Schoolmaster's tails may hang down a long time before they are tied fast to the chair again.

Alfred was fortunate to have enough family interest to get him entry to the Royal Navy College at Portsmouth, and to get in before it closed. He joined in May 1833 at the age of twelve and a half; the college closed in 1837 after which all budding officers proceeded directly to sea as described above. The closure of the College created a gap in officer training and in 1863 the wooden hulk *HMS Britannia* was moved to Dartmouth where it undertook the role of a cadet training ship; the Royal Navy's officer training academy is still based at Dartmouth retaining the name *HMS Britannia* until 1953 when it was renamed *HMS Dartmouth*, and the old name transferred to the newly launched royal yacht *HMY Britannia*.

Alfred was also lucky that Professor John Inman was the principal of the College during his time there. Inman, an ordained clergyman, was a brilliant naval scientist. At his suggestion, the Admiralty established a School of Naval Architecture at the College, so students became conversant with all the latest developments in shipbuilding, which in Alfred's time involved the use of steel and steam. As well as works on naval architecture, Inman also published works on mathematics, navigation, astronomy and gunnery. His 'Inman's Nautical Tables' on navigation and nautical astronomy remained in use for many years, in recognition of which he was elected a Fellow of the Royal Astronomical Society.

Under such a man, and in such an atmosphere, the studious and scientific Alfred could do nothing but thrive. As well as theoretical classroom studies, the students spent as much time as possible gaining practical experience – and learning to understand the breed of men that they would have under their command. Sailors were famously fearless of danger, fearless of the future, careless with their health, prepared to be taken in and skinned alive by all varieties of land shark and women, but equally generous with anything they possessed to any shipmate on hard times. A rough and ready group, close knit, god fearing, working aloft they sang and swore; they rarely blasphemed. Admiral Colomb (who would be Alfred's Flag Captain on the China Station) was later to recall

> *The men had great arms and shoulders. They could climb but they could not march. They had steady heads aloft, but very unsteady heads ashore. They were artisans in rope, leather and canvas. They were tailors, embroiderers, cooks and washer men. Nothing in them, or about them, had accurate limits. There was no greatness of soul that they might not ascend to; there was no temptation so light that they might not yield to it. They were artists, not mechanics; and being in constant interchange of combat and alliance with the uncertain and fickle elements of*

wind and weather, they were apt to think that everything that occurred was an emergency, so that they themselves partook of that emergency character.[19]

A tough learning experience for the son of a Bishop!

Alfred's letters to his mother show that he was already at sea in 1833, bound for Jamaica in the survey ship *HMS Thunderer*. The ship's log book records that before sailing *The Lord Bishop of Lichfield came onboard* at Chatham.

On the way to Madeira, he wrote to his mother at Garendon Park, Leicestershire, the home of her nephew Charles March-Phillipps[20], ...

> *Dear Mamma*
>
> *I commence writing my first letter from a foreign place. We hope to reach Madeira in 3 or 4 days. I have not been at all sick I am happy to say though we have had a rough sea and all the other youngsters have been sick as dogs. We set sail from Plymouth on Thursday last. I came up on deck to have my last sight of dear England, and was obliged to be at my station in the mizzen top for about half an hour reefing the sails next morning at half 5 o'clock.*

.... (took on provisions, including...) *8 dozen of beer which I like much better than that disgusting grog. I must assure you that I detest it....*
Sharks and grampus[21] have been seen.

> *(He....) witnessed a court martial of a man for using insolent language. We assembled with cocked hats and caps and with drawn sword to prevent the prisoner escaping. He was sentenced to receive 12 lashes on his back with a knotted rope. Afterwards he was released and laid on the table.*

In July 1839 Alfred passed the final difficult examination, and was appointed Mate on *HMS Imogene*, serving on the south-east coast of America in anti-slavery patrols. He won his commission as a lieutenant in 1841, one of the youngest officers in the Navy at the time. Sadly, his father did not live to see his success; the Bishop had died in 1836. In 1838 Sophia and the family had moved to their new home in Hambleden. One can only imagine her pride as Alfred stepped out of his carriage at the front door in his uniform, and how keen she would have been to show him off to the great and good in the village!

Alfred's next stroke of luck, or 'interest', occurred when his first posting was to the 42-gun frigate *HMS Belvedera* in the Mediterranean, commanded by Captain George Grey[22]. He served on the *Belvedera* until it was paid off in 1845. He must have done enough to satisfy Captain Grey, for in 1846 he was promoted to Commander, finding time in the year before taking up his next commission to publish three scientific treatises that demonstrated both his mathematical ability and his tendency to get bogged down in the detail, possibly at the expense of the principle. Nonetheless, although the style is ponderous to modern eyes, as practical, working manuals both were well received, and helped to establish his career as a 'thinking' officer. Quite remarkable when one considers he was only twenty-six.

The first was *Practical Rules for Determining the Course to be Steered to Escape from a Hurricane deduced from the Rotary Theory established by Colonel Reid* which was reviewed by the Naval and Military Gazette as follows

> *The author proceeds at once to his point and has not uttered a word more than is necessary. Indeed, we are assured that the Lords of the Admiralty will place a copy of it on board every vessel in Her Majesty's service. Lloyds should do the same by the mercantile marine.*

The paper contains remarkably detailed tables and diagrams of advice to captains, all calculated by hand!

The second was *On Ascertaining the Distance from Ships at Sea*; the Admiralty purchased the print run of 500 copies, which were *very usefully* used in ships chasing slavers off the coast of Africa. This treatise also includes hugely detailed tables, and a chapter on how a captain can ascertain the distance from another ship by recording the time between when the flash of the gun is observed and hearing its report, and multiply the time in seconds by 377. No spread sheets in those days!

The third was *'A pamphlet on the experimental cruizes* [sic] *of the line of battle ships in 1845: Containing the results of the trials, the method pursued to obtain them, ... of registering the necessary observations'*

Perhaps on the strength of these publications, in May the following year he was appointed commanding officer of the steam paddle ship *HMS Vixen* on the North American and West Indian Station, based at Bermuda under Vice Admiral Sir Francis Austen[23], and charged with disrupting the activities of slave traders and protecting British commercial interests. Vixen was what came to known as a 'gunboat'; she had a shallow draft, ideal for negotiating inlets and rivers to pursue slavers and pirates, sufficient gun power to deal with them, but with enough sail not to have to rely on coal on the open sea.

His first task, though, had nothing to do with chasing slavers and pirates. Much more mundanely he undertook the role of transporting the Duke of Palmella, one of the most important Portuguese diplomats and statesmen in the first half of the nineteenth century, from London, where he had been the Portuguese Ambassador, to Madeira. then he continued on to Mexico with the newly appointed British Ambassador, Percy Doyle. The journey took two and a half months. Such tasks were not difficult, but they were important, contributing, as they did, to the mosaic of imperial pride and to strengthening the illusion of inescapable British strength.

One might be forgiven for thinking that Alfred's somewhat meteoric career to this point had been guided by his family and their connections, but they had nothing to do with his next promotion.

Nicaragua was one of the strangest areas in Great Britain's informal empire. The British base was at Greytown, a miserable collection of huts at the mouth of the San Juan River. The Spanish had used the river to transport treasure down to the Caribbean, a trade which had attracted English pirates in the seventeenth century. For a brief moment of time, San Juan was the most important river in the world, which is why the British had taken it under their protection.

It had achieved fame of sorts when, in 1780, an ambitious young English naval captain, looking to make a name for himself by cutting the Spanish American Empire in two, rowed up the San Juan River from the Caribbean and trekked through the jungle to fool the Spanish by attacking their fortress at El Castillo from the landward side. The Spanish capitulated without much trouble, but the English soon found that disease was the real enemy. Only ten of the original two hundred survived, among them their leader, Horatio Nelson. The hill on which El Castillo stands is named Lomas de Nelson to this day.

Since then, apart from vague plans for a canal to the Pacific Ocean, Nicaragua had been deemed to be of little importance save as a refuge for slaves fleeing from Jamaica ………... until the discovery of gold in California in January 1848.

After that it became a vital link in the route from New York and New Orleans to the Pacific. Small boats transported passengers from Greytown up the San Juan River and across Lake Nicaragua. Then, mules, horses, or stagecoaches carried them over the small isthmus between the lake and the Pacific coast, where they would embark on ships to California. Long proposed plans for a canal suddenly assumed great importance, and the British saw Greytown as becoming one of the links in their chain of port cities that girdled the planet. With the United States showing more than a keen interest in the village, it was important that British influence was reinforced.

It was in this sensitive atmosphere that a local Nicaraguan commander kidnapped two British subjects in February 1848 and retreated thirty miles up the rapids and waterfalls of the fast-flowing, brown, caiman-infested San Juan river to a muddy, mosquito-ridden stockade called Serapique. What followed next is best described by Vice Admiral Austen, though not, perhaps, in the same flowing prose as his sister…….

On the morning of the 9th the expedition got under way and proceeded towards the fort. where it had been ascertained Colonel Salas was commanding officer. The settlement was about thirty miles up the river, which from the strength of the current and various rapids, is generally a four days' journey. Captain Loch and Commander Ryder proceeded to that place at once, with a force of 260 men in twelve boats, and after a most fatiguing pull of seventy-two hours, anchored on the evening of the 11th near the spot.

The post is situated on a point projecting into the river very abruptly to the height of 50 feet, is protected in the rear by a dense forest, and in the front by an abattis[24], formed of large trees felled, with their head and branches reaching into the river. The defences of the post consisted of six angular stockaded entrenchments, eight feet high and four feet thick, one side of each stockade looking across the river, and the other down the reach. The principal stockade commanded the landing place, in which one of the guns was mounted at the time.

On Friday, the 12th instant, Captain Loch and Commander Ryder (who were in advance in their gigs) hove in sight of Serapaqui, situated at the head of a straight reach of about a mile and a half long. No sooner did their boat appear, than she was fired upon by two guns.

As this act effectually prevented any peaceable arrangements, Captain Loch and Commander Ryder determined that the stockade could only to be approached by heading a rapid current of nearly five knots an hour (stet) in order to pass the fort and descend towards a steep and narrow landing place above the stockaded batteries. Boats were at once brought up, but the current was so strong, that one hour and forty minutes elapsed before they were enabled to pass the batteries sufficiently high to drop down to the landing place previously mentioned, by which time nearly all the boats were up.

It was with great satisfaction that I can report the cool and steady behaviour of the men, under the trying circumstances of crowded boats, exposed to a hot fire, from both sides of the river, from unseen marksmen, without the possibility of effectually returning it, while in almost a stationary position, owing to the current running like a mill-stream. And it is astonishing to me that a greater loss did not occur, as the boats were riddled with shot, and nearly half the oars broken.

Captain Loch then gave the order to land. The boats' crews charged upwards with an English cheer. Their sheer determination intimidated the enemy – their cutlasses and pistols proved devastating, as so often, in the hands of well-trained and well-disciplined men. Within ten minutes our flag was hoisted in the fort.

The Nicaraguan troops fled at once. After a chase of thirty minutes into the thick woods, Captain Loch ordered the recall to be sounded, destroyed the stockades, spiked the guns, broke their trunnions, and threw them into the river, together with muskets, ammunition; and, after embarking, the force set fire to the defences.

The loss on our side amounted to two killed, and one officer and twelve seamen, marines, and soldiers, wounded. Captain Loch was unable to ascertain accurately the loss of the enemy, owing to the density of the cover into which they retreated: twenty, however, were found dead, and I have reason to believe that about double the number were wounded. Nine prisoners were captured, amongst them two wounded officers. Their force consisted of about 200 soldiers, besides some boatmen, pressed by Colonel Salas into his service.

To distinguish one brave officer from another, when all did their duty, is a difficult task; but I may remark, that Captain Smith, commanding the detachment of her Majesty's 38th Regiment; Commander Ryder, at the head of his division, close by Captain Loch ; Lieutenants Johnson and Ridge, of the 'Alarm', leading their men in gallant style ; and First Lieutenant Boyle, Royal Marines, of the same ship, leading his detachment as the captain's guard, and showing an example which his marines could not but follow.

Alfred was not concerned with honours and promotions; he was just pleased to have seen some action. He wrote to his mother....

> We were under heavy fire from about 200 men for more than an hour- the whizzing and hissing and popping was not pleasant, but I was glad to find that I retained my presence of mind and was able to laugh at the shots as they whizzed by me. We had 2 men killed and 13 wounded.

However, although *probably there did not exist as his contemporary a less ambitious man than himself*[25], for his *brilliant service at the capture of Fort Serapique*[26], and, not least, for demonstrating the assertiveness in dealings with foreigners required by recently appointed Foreign Secretary Lord Palmerston, he was promoted to the rank of captain – a monarch within his ship.

A captain's power was not absolute, but nearly so. He could not declare war – at least not against a European power. He could not sentence a man to death and could not have him flogged without recording it. When in company with other ships he had to obey instructions from the senior officer of the flotilla – who could come aboard anytime to inspect and comment on his ship and his company. Ships at all times had to be ready for inspection. When sailing alone he would have had his orders, yet these could be little more than general directives. He was expected to make his own decisions; he had few constraints. Consequently, captains were invariably members of the upper class as it was an accepted maxim that only men from that stratum of society possessed the charisma and other leadership qualities that allowed them to feel comfortable with command.

A captain would come aboard to the shrill and quaver of a Boatswain's pipe, the Marine guard snapped to attention, assembled officers uncovered their heads, and the crew stood rigid. Except on urgent matters, he was not addressed unless he made the first approach. On being addressed by the captain, a crew member would whip off his hat while in the same movement removing the ubiquitous wad of chewing tobacco in his mouth. Once the conversation was over, he would replace both in the same movement.

Alfred described something of his life as a captain in his letters to his son. He complained about never going to bed when at sea. He wrote home…

> …*I haven't been to bed since we left England. I only lie in my clothes. With big ships sailing so close together, I have to be up in a second*[27].

And again

> …*you may think of Papa in a thick rough jacket, spyglass slung around his neck, cap on his head lying down on a sofa and perhaps just beginning a nap when an officer comes in and says 'the Admiral's ship has just made a signal 'Tack in Succession'*[28]

The captain was an individual. Rendered more than usually individualistic by his lonely position and his unbounded powers, he could make or break a ship. His personality was therefore all-important. From all accounts, Alfred was….

> …. *immovable as a disciplinarian. Law was law in his view, and it would not strike him that it was not to proceed. In such things he was apt to regard himself as a machine, and to discharge from his mind everything that might hinder its efficient working. But he had that great quality in a commander of trusting, and letting it be known that he did so. As a consequence, he was always very well served, and without any apparent force on his part, all under his command felt pressed to make it a success. Few who served with him have not some grateful recollection of a difficulty smoothed, a trouble got over, an encouraging and sympathetic word or letter or some kind help given.*[29]

Contemporaries were often tempted to think that such apparent geniality and even temperament meant that he lacked firmness. On the contrary, he would let nothing stand in his way if he deemed an action to be right – he neither craved affection from his crew, nor saw a virtue in their disaffection. A certain *rigid rectitude of mind* meant that he saw things in black and white; there was the right way and the wrong way and hang the consequences. It made all who had dealings with him feel absolutely safe – they knew exactly where they stood; in particular those in the Admiralty, who proceeded to promote him regularly over the next thirty-seven years until he had attained the highest rank possible in the Royal Navy.

This *rigid rectitude of mind* was not unique to Alfred: it was symptomatic of the Victorian Navy as a whole. As it grappled with the conversion from oak and canvas to steel and turbines, the Admiralty tended to place process over product, method over initiative. It was a battle between centralisation and delegation – the temptation was to rely on naval technologists (of which Alfred and his friend Captain Philip Colomb were but two) who claimed that they had 'solved' problems when they really hadn't. How could they? That there had been no major fleet action in a generation was discussed, but rarely with concern. In truth, the balance of thought in the Navy got out of kilter. Individualism and craft lore were being replaced by standardised training and scientific experiment, and the twin attendants of the industrial age, regimentation and specialisation, became engrained in the culture of the Navy. Yes, it was difficult integrating new concepts and technologies into a peacetime navy, but in coping with it, centralised command, routine and inertia took precedence over the individual flair needed in battle – as was to be discovered when the Navy was required to defeat a serious enemy after 1914. Although the risks of understating the *paramount importance* of the human element and the tendency to underestimate the enemy had been pointed out in 1907 by Admiral Sir Cyprian Bridge[30], British losses at Jutland and the failure to destroy the German fleet were arguably due to a culture of timidity and subservience to manuals that had developed over the Victorian and Edwardian periods. Process had superseded product.

5

In Sickness and in Health

Whoso findeth a wife findeth a good thing, and obtaineth favour of the Lord.

Proverbs 18:22

Alfred's command of the *Vixen* concluded in May 1848; he would have to wait five years for another command. The country he arrived back to was not a happy place – class war and imminent revolution were openly discussed. The Government was severely exercised by civil unrest on the Continent and the activities of the Chartists at home. In fact, Alfred's return coincided with the last, rather sad demonstration of the Chartists on Kennington Common. The rally was badly organised; there was heavy rain on the day, and the movement ended as rather a damp squib.

Paradoxically, 1848 marked the end of the poor harvests and economic downturns that had begun in the aftermath of Waterloo, and national morale was beginning to improve. It was lifted further in 1850 when, as Foreign secretary, Lord Palmerston, controversially sent ships to blockade Greece to seek retribution from the alleged attack on a British resident of Athens. When asked to defend his action in Parliament, he rather fancifully insisted that Britain had avoided the continental revolutions of 1848 because of its social structure, which uniquely combined respect for the established order with widespread opportunities for self-help. It was a society in which all Britons might aspire to better themselves and rise up the social scale….

> *We have shown the example of a nation, in which every class of society accepts with cheerfulness the lot which Providence has assigned to it; while at the same time every individual of each class is constantly striving to raise himself in the social scale —*

not by injustice and wrong, not by violence and illegality — but by persevering good conduct, and by the steady and energetic exertion of the moral and intellectual faculties with which his Creator has endowed him.

To this remarkably stable yet fluid social structure, Palmerston continued, was allied an equally unrivalled capacity to project national power overseas, and it was therefore up to Parliament to decide….

.... whether, as the Roman, in days of old, held himself free from indignity, when he could say Civis Romanus sum; so also, a British subject, in whatever land he may be, shall feel confident that the watchful eye and the strong arm of England, will protect him against injustice and wrong.[31]

Complacent and exaggerated depictions of the British social structure and foreign policy these may have been, but they reflected the view of the country's grandees, including Sir George Grey who, as Home Secretary, was in the Cabinet with Palmerston – and by extension his brother-in-law, Alfred.

It was therefore a good time to be British (well actually, English), wealthy and in the navy. Even more so as in 1849 the Government had repealed the Navigation Acts[32], which, combined with the earlier repeal of the Corn Laws, represented the final establishment of free trade worldwide for all and the triumph of new industrialists over landed interests.

Britain could do this because it was confident the system was loaded in its favour - it was the workshop and financier of the world, and it had the world's most powerful navy to act as a global policeman. Although the reforms opened up markets for British goods everywhere and enabled Britain to import cheap foreign goods, most importantly raw materials and foodstuffs to fuel industrial expansion, in fact all countries benefited from Royal Navy protection against pirates, and so could see benefits for themselves. Consequently, Britain's maritime role enabled her to get some official support for, and grudging unofficial respect of, Pax Britannia from much of the world.

But the Navy's ability to exert its power with impunity around the world had to rest on secure foundations. As ever, the key to success was absolute security at home, in other words complete control of the Channel and the Western Approaches. As so often in the history of modern Britain, military planners and statesmen had to grapple with the problem of maintaining a worldwide empire while defending the home islands. The ability and readiness of the navy to achieve these goals depended on its willingness to respond to developments in naval technology – which in the mid-nineteenth century meant steam.

Although Britain led the world in land-based steam technology, and although the advantages of steam at sea were obvious – reduced dependence on wind, predictable journey times, increased manoeuvrability making it easier to navigate inshore and in hazardous waters, and to attack enemy ships in anchorages - the Navy was slow to adapt to it. Admiral Philip Colomb remembered…

> *Without doubt, it was…. the most natural thing in the world that a fleet should be composed of sailing ships, screw ships and paddle ships. The belief that sailing ships were to go, and that paddles were almost gone would have been impossible to inculcate. All minds…. would consider how the heterogeneous elements could best be combined…. the idea was to maintain intact the line-of-battle -ship, frigate and slop of the old days, only more perfect…*[33]

The Admiralty, and the nation, viewed their navy with rose-tinted nostalgia. Admiral Charles Cooper Penrose-Fitzgerald, in a lecture to the Royal United Services Institution in 1887 would bemoan…

> *Evolutions aloft are so attractive and so showy; there is so much swagger about them. Our Admirals have always so highly commended and attached so much value to the smart shifting of topsails or topgallant sails, and so many lieutenants have worked their promotions out of the successful cultivation of this sort of seamanship….that we seem to have lost sight of the fact*

that it has nothing to do with fighting efficiently in the present day.

The transition to steam was encapsulated beautifully by Turner in his 1838 masterpiece, possibly the single most popular painting of a warship in the history of British art, *The Fighting Temaraire*[34], in which the proud, ghostly hulk that had seen distinguished service at Trafalgar, is depicted being dragged ignominiously, ironically by a dirty steam tugboat, to be broken up for scrap. The sun setting symbolises the end of an epoch in the history of the British Royal Navy.

Initially, Britain converted sailing ships to steam by dropping in an engine and a propeller. However, the French seemed superior in mastering the new technology, and ordered the world's first purpose-built steam powered battleship, *Napoleon*, which was launched in 1850[35]. The Admiralty had to respond. *HMS Agamemnon* was launched in 1852 and the 3-decker *HMS Duke of Wellington in 1853*; both were purpose-built screw driven battleships. But because the engines were inefficient, only to be used in emergencies and in battle, the ships had a full complement of masts and sails and looked every bit like the proud warships of Hawke, Howe and Nelson. The only difference to the casual observer was the chimney protruding fore of the mainmast and the increased length to make room for the engine. The engine had arrived, but this was still a sailing navy.

Wooden battleships, though, were now vulnerable to improved armaments like exploding shells...........so the race was on to build an iron-armoured battleship. As ever, the French led the way. In 1858 news arrived that she was building the world's first ironclads - *La Gloire*, *Invincible* and *Normandie*. The British response was *HMS Warrior*, ordered in May 1859 and commissioned in August 1861. Alfred commented, rather enigmatically, about her in a letter home…

I wonder if you have been told of the new Iron Ships that are being built, of immense size and weight. One, the first, is just finished and is called the Warrior, and I am rather afraid that

*we may have to be sent out to have a cruise with her, and go
and look for a gale to see how she answers in bad weather.*[36]

Almost twice as large, faster and with more firepower than *La Gloire*,
Warrior determined that the struggle to control the Channel was over.
She was the ultimate deterrent. The French might innovate, but the British
always bettered the design, and in a shorter space of time. The ability to
build more and faster than anyone else, the virtual monopoly of the best
stoking coal, immense financial resources, and the sheer experience and
professionalism of the crews all combined to enable Britain to retain
maritime mastery for the rest of the century.

Not that mastery came easily. Older officers were not conditioned to
change; neither training nor experience had given them any expectation
that the introduction of novelties like engines or shell guns would
necessarily alter the fundamentals of sea warfare, and the idea that they
should seek technical change to gain advantage was actually repugnant.
They were used to the advantages of geography - being to the west of
Europe gave British sailors the advantage of prevailing westerly winds in
wartime, for the very winds which carried them to the enemy kept the
enemy penned in his harbours. Moreover....

> *There was a very strong and universal feeling that it was not
> seamanlike to use steam, except perhaps in a flat calm, and that
> any Captain that could not take his ship in or out of harbour
> under sail with a commanding breeze was 'no seaman'; it was
> scarcely possible to make a more scathing and derogatory
> remark against him. It would have been scarcely worse for his
> professional reputation to say that 'he drinks'.*

> *And another reason was the remarkable parsimony on behalf
> of the Admiralty in the use of coal. Captains were over and
> over again hauled over the coals (no pun intended) for failing to
> exercise economy in the use of coal*[37].

Nevertheless, something was happening. It was only dimly perceived at
first, but soon became unmistakable: industrial technology and invention

was taking over from knowledge of winds and tides, of crossing the T[38], of mastery of short-range gunnery. After fifty years of rather complacent superiority, the country was now in an arms race, conditions that encouraged a new kind of officer - one who was excited by technical challenges and who grasped eagerly at new possibilities.

Such an officer was Alfred. Fortunately, he was young enough and bright enough to grasp the possibilities. His personality exactly reflected the characteristics of high-Victorian England – the emphasis on thought, work and progress. Clear thinking was preferred to impulse or prejudice, and the battle of ideas to the dictatorships of slogans; hard work was considered the foundation of all material advancement; and both hard work and clear thinking were deemed essential to continued national progress. The corollary was, of course, that the stress on thought, work and progress carried with it smugness, dullness and cant; it also was accompanied by a heightened sense of national pride and hubristic self-confidence, qualities that found expression in the Great Exhibition of 1851.

Although the project was enthusiastically promoted by Prince Albert, it's proposed site in Hyde Park[39] was initially met with widespread opposition on the grounds that it would damage the trees, the flowers and the lawns, and that it would lead to the influx of domestic and foreign undesirables in the very heart of the city (plus ça change!). Such resistance having been overcome, the story goes that with only days to go before the Exhibition was to open, the enormous building became overrun with sparrows whose droppings were not complementing the exhibits. The powers that be were at a loss about what to do, until Queen Victoria called for the elderly Duke of Wellington, who apparently listened carefully to the distraught Queen and then calmly replied 'Sparrow hawks, Ma'am'. The problem was solved in an instant and, to the relief of all, the Great Exhibition was opened by the Queen on time on 1 May, in the presence of a glittering array of international visitors and national worthies – including Home Secretary Sir George Grey, his wife and his wife's mother escorted by her son, Captain Alfred Ryder, resplendent in his dress uniform. It was a vast building – a glass cathedral, more than half a kilometre in length[40], high enough to enclose elm trees to demonstrate man's triumph over nature. Nothing like it had ever been seen before anywhere in the world. It was truly a public expression of Britain's prowess. Crowds flocked to the Crystal Palace[41] as it came to be known, travelling on the new railway system[42]; when it closed six months later, it was estimated that it had been seen by one-fifth of the entire population of Britain[43]. In popularity perhaps only the 2012 Olympic Games in London can rival it.

And just like the Games, the Exhibition gave the country a chance to show off. It was a statement to the country and to the world of British achievement, not only as an industrial power, but a world power – an imperial power. It sought to proclaim the triumph of free trade and to symbolise the end of the often divisive and difficult experiences of the 1830s and 1840s, notably the contentious repeal of the corn laws and attempts to reform Parliament by broadening the franchise. Incidentally, the debate over the repeal of the Corn Laws, which split the Conservative Party and kept them out of power for a generation, has a modern resonance (as I write) with the question of whether Britain should be in a Customs Union with the European Union. Only time will tell whether the current debate will have a similar political outcome.

Popular highlights of the exhibition included the fountain at the centre of the building, twenty-seven feet high and made from four tons of pink glass; another fountain provided tourists with an endless stream of Schweppes mineral water (a representation of the Exhibition fountain can still be seen on bottles of their tonic water). The Indian section introduced visitors for the first time to the richness and quality of Indian textiles, but was particularly remembered for the howdah displayed on a stuffed elephant. The world's largest known diamond, the Koh-i-Noor was on show, as was a collection of stuffed animals arranged in tableaux, such as kittens taking tea and a frog having a shave!

Although the Crystal Palace is now long gone[44], we continue to benefit from its success and to reflect on the tangible evidence of Victorian pomp. The surplus that the Exhibition accumulated was used to acquire land in South Kensington on which would be constructed the Victoria and Albert Museum, the Science Museum, the Natural History Museum, Imperial

College, the Royal Albert Hall and other institutions. This commitment to science, the applied arts, education and design was Prince Albert's abiding legacy, and no member of the royal family since has made so many-sided a contribution to the cultural and intellectual life of the United Kingdom.

Into this paean of science and education tip-toed Alfred, who in 1852 published the rather snappily titled

> *A treatise on economy of fuel: showing how it may be attained on board men-of-war steamers; and pointing out the considerations which should be carefully studied when engines are being ordered for steamers-of-war, mail packets, or merchant ships in order that their respective duties may be performed with the least possible consumption of fuel.*

He described himself on the title page as a *late student at the Royal Naval College, Portsmouth* – a title that must have carried a certain cachet. He rather modestly advised his readers that….

> *….in introducing the following treatise to his brother officers, the writer has no other wish than it may prove useful to them until it is supplanted by some other with greater claims on their confidence.*

By the early 1840s France felt ready to attempt to flex its muscles to recover prestige lost in the Napoleonic Wars. News came of the growth of the French marine and the completion of the defences at Cherbourg, making the port its first battleship base in the Channel and an arsenal for invasion. So, in this context and in that of the race to build the biggest and best ironclad, one can see the importance of Alfred's book in educating the navy. He described it as being aimed at….

> *…. officers who may have been prevented from availing themselves of the opportunities of studying steam as the main source of power when they were at Portsmouth and Woolwich.*

It was a small, though important, contribution to the professionalism of the Royal Navy that enabled it to keep ahead of its rivals.

As a successful young officer with prospects, Alfred needed a wife. As a serving sailor, he had few opportunities to meet suitable young women. Fortunately, his mother's sister had an attractive eighteen-year-old daughter, Louisa (Louie), whom both families considered eminently eligible - Alfred's brother, William, wrote to her wishing her 'hearty good wishes and affection' on her forthcoming marriage.

The couple had met in London when Louie was staying with her grandparents at their residence in Wimpole Street. Alfred later visited her at her family home at Launde Abbey in Leicestershire, a manor house that was (still is) used as a Christian retreat. They married in June 1852 at the medieval parish church of the quiet hamlet of Loddington, Leicestershire and set up home in the Deanery at Lichfield. Ten months later they were overjoyed when their son Edward (Eddy) was born.

Sadly, Alfred had very little time to enjoy his family for in December 1853 he took command of *HMS Dauntless*, a steam-driven 24-gun (later increased to 33) frigate. As the Times reported….

> *Their Lordships have acted wisely in placing the Dauntless under the command of so talented and popular an officer as Captain Ryder. From the order, discipline and good feeling which existed on board his previous vessel, the Vixen, there is every prospect of the Dauntless being a happy and well-regulated ship.*

Initially the *Dauntless* was attached to the strategically important Channel Squadron, but this duty was interrupted by the outbreak of hostilities in the Crimea.

Like all wars, the reasons behind it are clouded in smoke and mirrors, but one never goes far wrong by following the money. Russia was the least popular of all the European powers as far as British public opinion was concerned, because of its autocratic government, and its savage treatment of liberals who vainly campaigned for domestic reform (often from their exiled homes in London).

The British believed, rightly or wrongly, that Russia had designs on the Ottoman Empire, and beyond that, on India. Inevitably, then, they seized the chance to cut Russia down to size as soon as the opportunity presented itself. So, what has changed since then, you may wonder? Russian intentions are rightly still viewed with suspicion in the West; an unpredictable United States has replaced Britain as the international ringmaster, but the part of the world where west meets east, where Christians meet Muslims, where Shia meets Sunni, is still a flashpoint, and is scarcely ever out of the news for all the wrong reasons.

In 1853 a series of scuffles about the treatment of Christians in Ottoman controlled Moldavia and Wallachia (roughly the equivalent of modern Romania) was quickly and deliberately escalated until a substantial British force was dispatched to the Black Sea, where it was joined by the French who were anxious about protecting their own extensive business interests in Constantinople, Aleppo and Damascus, and were prepared to put their maritime rivalry with Britain on hold. The aim was simple: Russia was to be taught a lesson. If Palmerston was to have his way, it would lead to the total dismemberment of Russia.

The Crimean War is remembered primarily for the failings and heroism of the army, the compassion of nurses and the blunders of generals and that Britain managed to snatch victory from the jaws of defeat. The role of the Navy is barely mentioned and one may imagine its role was insignificant – though not, I suspect, to those who were on the receiving end of Russian shells. In fact, the first actions of the war were fought not in the Crimea, but in the Baltic, where Admiral Sir Charles Napier led the largest fleet that the Royal Navy had assembled since the Napoleonic Wars with the purpose of bottling up the Russian fleet and attacking harbours where possible. The mission was to prove acrimonious. For a start, Napier, although a hero of several actions in the War of 1812 (with the United States), the Napoleonic Wars and the Syrian War, was seventy years old, increasingly volatile and somewhat past his prime. The public, however, was pleased at the appointment of probably the most charismatic admiral of the time and *indulged in the most extravagant expectations as to what the squadron under his command would shortly accomplish.*[45] They were to be disappointed. Napier found it difficult to find crews for his fleet – he commented *never, perhaps, had finer ships left our shores; yet never before* had a squadron sailed so deplorably manned[46]. Arriving in the Baltic he made the following much criticised signal to his command....

> Lads, war is declared with a numerous and bold enemy. Should they meet us and offer battle, you know how to dispose of them. Should they remain in port, we must try and get at them. Success depends upon the quickness and precision of your firing. Also, lads, sharpen your cutlasses, and the day is your own!

Hardly the command in an age of steam!

As it turned out, the Russians did not dare to come out of their harbours (why would they – to fight the strongest navy in the world?), and a stalemate followed. As Alfred wrote to his brother, Richard, *The Russians keep very snug and quiet in their batteries[47]*; consequently, Napier could not deliver the stirring victory demanded of him by the Admiralty and the public, and his ships' crews had a very dull time gazing at enemy forts. Dauntless spent ten weeks cruising up and down the coast, reconnoitring the Russian fleet in harbour, taking soundings and sketching batteries, ships and dockyards.

Alfred wrote to his brother in May, quite homesick....

> How beautiful the leaves and buds must be looking in dear old England. Louie tells me she and the wee baby were most happy on their visit to Hambleden.

At the end of the summer, greatly disappointed and frustrated, the fleet returned to Britain, though not before Napier had threatened to court martial Alfred and his fellow captain, Henry Codrington for failing to achieve the required standards. The Admiralty refused to support this course of action as both officers were sufficiently well connected to prevent any action being taken against them[48], and eventually it was Napier himself who was controversially recalled.

As the Clerk at the Admiralty wrote to Alfred....

> *My Dear Ryder*
>
> *My hands are now untied. And I send you the mysterious document from Sir Chas, Napier. I longed to give you all the information I could, but as the correspondence has been carried on in this department, I could not do more than give a hint to Lady Grey. I most sincerely hope and believe that you will get the better of your much-respected Commander in Chief. His letter is a mere petulant effusion and I do not think has much weight here. I am very glad that the Admiralty have behaved like gentlemen, and informed you of what is going on.*

Dauntless was then ordered to join the fleet in the siege of Sebastopol, Russia's prime Black Sea port. The army had tried to take the port from the landward side, but engagements at Balaclava (notoriously) and Inkerman proved inconclusive, and the army was left to face the Crimean winter that was invariably Russia's most deadly and reliable ally. Alfred wrote home in March 1856 that *the ice was so thick that I could almost walk on shore from the ship this morning.*[49]To the deaths and casualties arising from the incompetence of senior British commanders, were added the scourges of cholera, dysentery and other virulent diseases, which reached epidemic proportions and threatened to wipe out the allied forces completely. The sick and wounded were tended by the zealous and energetic Florence Nightingale, which would grant her a legendry reputation as the 'lady with the lamp'. Alfred's letter home from Constantinople in December 1854 refers to Miss Nightingale as being….

> *very good looking. I wonder the man who did the Chorister Boys (?) does not get up a picture of the English nurse bending over the wounded soldiers – Miss N would make a beautiful picture and he would make his fortune.* (my question mark)

He also refers to a sketch he made of the harbour at Balaclava[50], which is reproduced in this volume.

Perhaps unsurprisingly, no mention is made of Mary Seacole, the pioneering British-Jamaican business woman and nurse. After funding her own passage to the Crimea, she established the British Hotel near Balaclava to provide 'a mess-table and comfortable quarters for sick and convalescent officers'. She also visited the battlefield, sometimes under fire, to nurse the wounded, and became known as 'Mother Seacole'. Her reputation rivalled that of Florence Nightingale.

Another letter records that….

> …. our splendid cavalry is extinguished or soon will be as far as their losses are concerned. We shall have to mount all the troopers afresh from England in the Spring. You must not suppose that the officers are in bad heart. They will be very glad when it is all over, but look forward to getting into Sebastopol before long.

Eventually, a combination of naval bombardment and renewed army activity finally conquered Sebastopol in September 1855, and the Peace of Paris brought the war to an end on March 30, 1856.

Sadly, Alfred would not take part in the victory celebrations. While he was in the Black Sea, Louie was dying of consumption and to have the best chance of seeing her husband before death, and possibly in the hope that a change of climate might cure her, she went to Malta. Alfred knew it would likely be too late for him to see her before she died, but as he wrote to his commanding officer Admiral Sir Edmund Lyons….

> ……I must not fail to attempt it. I am well aware that resigning the command of a ship, even in peacetime is prejudicial to an officer's character, and that in time of war it can only be justified by circumstances of so unusual a character as to be of rare occurrence. But I have decided on a course of conduct which is my duty to pursue under the peculiar circumstances of my case.

But he arrived too late; she had died on 10th October 1855 aged 22, leaving Eddy at just two and a half. In all, Alfred and Louie had been married for forty months, though their actual time together had been little more than eighteen months. They had barely time to get to know each other, and Alfred was heartbroken. Losing a spouse can be devastating - one day you are married; the next day you are single, alone, and grieving. We can assume that Alfred felt completely numb and lost, but what really consumed his soul was anger. It was if his world had come to a halt. His hopes for the future were shattered.

Today we understand that it takes time before one can begin to feel a sense of normality after the death of a spouse – especially one so desperately young. The pain does not just disappear nor will it heal itself. Today we accept that grieving has to go through certain definite stages which cannot be rushed - denial and isolation, anger, guilt, depression before final acceptance. Each of us may spend different lengths of time working through these steps and we may all experience each stage with different levels of intensity. Moreover, the four stages of grieving do not necessarily occur in any specific order, but they do all have to be dealt with before one is able to move on. Alfred, sadly, was not afforded the luxury of the time required to work through the stages of grief, nor the time to go through the grieving process with his loved ones – his mother and Louie's parents. Within six weeks he had rejoined the fleet.

It seems likely that he not been able to work through his feelings of anger, guilt and depression –the tragedy of the loss of his wife would haunt him for the rest of his life and would eventually contribute to his death. Her untimely demise planted the first seeds of doubt in his faith. Why had God punished him, and his family, so cruelly? He contemplated how one could believe deeply in the existence of a deity, but then lose that faith after the untimely loss of the one's closest and dearest. He would never forgive himself for not being beside her in her final days, and he would treasure their son in her memory. Yet the pain of his loss would mean he developed a more empathetic understanding of people – an understanding that would be the basis of the social causes that would occupy him during the latter stages of his life.

She is buried in Malta in a grave designed by Alfred, bearing the inscription 'Thy Will be Done.'

Alfred's service on behalf of Turkey, though relatively brief, was later[51] to be recognised by the award of the Order of the Medjidie by Sultan

Abdülmecid to members of the British Army, the Royal Navy and the French Army as a reward for distinguished service during the Crimean War. As his only decoration for action in wartime, and though the order was issued in great numbers, Alfred was considerably proud of the award.

Apparently forgiven by Admiral Lyons, he rejoined the *Dauntless* at the end of November, and would stay with her on patrol in the Mediterranean and the Black Sea for the next fifteen months till March 1857, albeit with occasional short periods of home leave. It was during this period that Alfred started writing to his son, Eddy, at his grandmother's house at Launde Abbey. The delightful letters are beautifully illustrated with drawings and watercolours; they provide a fascinating commentary on the life of a Captain, and a most touching and human insight into Alfred's mind. I urge you to read them[52].

It is perhaps worth reproducing the first letter, dated 8 March 1856, when Eddy was just three, as it sets the tone for the rest….

My dear Baby,

Uncle Tom[53] sends Baby a picture which he has drawn of Papa's beautiful big dog Sailor. He is such a good kind dog that Papa hopes one day to bring him to England for Baby to play with. He will be so fond of Baby, if Baby will pat him and stroke him and love him very much.

He comes to see Papa and Uncle Tom every morning at breakfast. They put a piece of toast on his nose and then say one-two-three and when they have said three, he tosses up his head and catches the toast in the air and eats it. The poor dog has been very lame. He was running about on the shore and he trod on a piece of glass which cut his foot very badly. He has not been able to have a good run on shore for many days, but his foot is much better now.

Uncle Tom is going today to try and shoot an owl and if he can kill one, he will get it stuffed and send it home for Baby. There are a great many large owls on the shore with horns on their heads, not horns like cows, but all feathers. These owls are very fierce and kill a great many other birds, and the young hares[54].

Dear Papa is very well. He has had a great deal to do lately, for the weather has been very stormy and the wind is blowing very hard, and Papa has been up on deck most of the night, to take care of the ship, and has got very little sleep. It is fine weather now, but very cold.

Papa sends much love to his dear little boy and so does Uncle Tom to Baby.

From the Irish Channel, Alfred wrote…

I made a very pretty excursion while we were at Queenstown[55] up the Blackwater above Youghal to Lismore.

The first seven miles had to be performed on Irish Jaunting Cars. They are capital carriages for fine weather and the daytime, but as you all sit outside it is very clear that if the weather is bad you stand a good chance of getting wet. And as one generally likes to turn one's head towards the view of the country we are driving to, one's neck gets such a twist in it from looking sideways, that it makes it quite sore. Besides which one's legs are in great danger from any other car passing by, so there is no protection from them. And as to taking a nap on them it is impossible, as you are very likely to be jerked off if the car turns short round a corner.

The river scenery was very pretty, something like the Rhine where you and I hope to go with our knapsacks some day.

The letters were full of affection for Eddy. From Tangier in October 1856, when Eddy was three and a half, he wrote…

*Papa sends plenty of kisses to Eddy • • • • • • • • • • • • • • • •.
Papa will kiss all those round spots when they are dry and Eddy may kiss then again.[56]*

Alfred would continue to write to Eddy till 1868, from places as afar as Sinope (where he wrote about hunting bustards), Gibraltar, Tangier (with details of a wild boar hunt), Messina (including a story of how a seaman, one Emmanuel Charles, *a very odd name is it not*, fell from the top of the 100ft mast, and *broke his leg all to pieces, which would have to have it amputated. Won't that be very sad to have to hop on one leg for the rest of his life.'*) Another letter from Messina refers to a dinner with an American *who talked through his nose like American gentlemen generally do.* From Malta, Alfred wrote of how he took some of the officers on a twenty mile walk across the island – to his *friend the Governor* where they had dinner and *picked oranges off the trees, but they were oh so sour.* Then they walked twenty miles back!

No, this was not a holiday cruise; it was part of the Royal Navy's responsibilities to maintain British interests and to counter the efforts of rivals!

The *Dauntless* was paid off in March 1857. Alfred took particular pleasure in the beautiful communion service of plate presented by the gun-room officers to the Chaplain *as a kind friend and a Christian minister.* He also took great satisfaction in arranging for the Admiralty to give….

> *….orders that the restrictions hitherto observed with regard to smoking on board a man of war alongside the dockyard jetty are to be removed - and that for the first time within half a century the boon has been conceded to 'poor Jack' to smoke his 'baccy' in comfort, whether alongside the dockyard or afloat.*
>
> *The inspecting officer gave his approval in unqualified terms as to the discipline and efficiency of the ship's company.*[57]

Alfred returned to Hambleden with the ship's dog, Sailor, by way of the newly opened Henley branch line, in time to be home for the birth of his niece Una, daughter of sister-in-law Julia who was living at the Cottage while her husband, Spencer[58], was serving in India with the Bengal Light Infantry. These were happy days for Alfred, playing ball and hide-and-seek with his four-year-old son, walking through the woods and fields with him, taking him to the mill at Mill End to watch the barges taking the flour up and down the river, and of course, spending time with his mother and extended family.

He was to stay in Hambleden until his next commission, *HMS Hero* in 1861.

6

Seeing the Light

And I gave my heart to seek and search out by wisdom
concerning all things that are done under heaven.

Ecclesiastes 1:13

It is difficult to overestimate the extent to which the British, after the defeat of Napoleon, continued to feel paranoia about the French. Not only did all the English military, and many of their politicians, continue to believe that the greatest political threat came from France (up to and including the Crimean War, when the French and English were supposedly allies – Lord Raglan, commander of the British troops, insisted on referring to the defenders of Sebastopol as 'the French', for the last time he had been in combat was on the fields of Waterloo). Not only did Palmerston and Wellington fear the prospect of a French invasion long after the possibility of such an event had been extinguished, but France was also seen as the very object lesson of what could happen if a society imploded. National anxiety had increased when the French built the world's first ironclad battleship, *La Gloire*, in 1858, an event that precipitated an arms race between the two nations that only ended in 1860 with the commissioning of *HMS Warrior* in 1861.

In 1859 it was believed that the ominously named Napoleon III was planning an invasion. He was thought to be too unstable to permit his pacific assurances to be taken on trust. The French had already completed the defences of Cherbourg, making the port its first battleship base in the Channel and an arsenal for invasion, a base for a 'steam bridge' across the Channel - to which the British had responded by building up steam fleet bases at Alderney and Portland. Nonetheless, there were doubts that even being the predominant sea power would not prevent an invasion, given

Britain's global commitments; doubts which created anxiety regarding the country's inviolability from overseas attack.

As Lord Palmerston wrote to Gladstone in December 1859....

> *It is quite clear that if by sudden attack by an Enemy landed in strength our Dock-yards were to be destroyed our Maritime Power would for more than half a century be paralysed, and our Colonies, our commerce, and the Subsistence of a large Part of our Population would be at the Mercy of our Enemy, who would be sure to shew us no Mercy—we should be reduced to the Rank of a third Rate Power if no worse happened to us. That such a Landing is in the present State of Things possible must be manifest. No Naval Force of ours can effectually prevent it. ... One night is enough for the Passage to our Coast, and Twenty Thousand men might be landed at any Point before our Fleet knew that the Enemy was out of Harbour.*

So, in line with the recommendations of the 1860 Royal Commission on the Defence of the United Kingdom and disregarding the traditional doctrine of command of the seas, the Government invested heavily in a series of coastal fortifications – the so called 'Palmerston Follies', echoing the chain of Martello towers built during the Napoleonic Wars. At the same time, over 150,000 burghers and country dwellers were enrolled with much enthusiasm into a much-expanded militia. The exact military worth of these measures is hard to assess, especially as around Portsmouth they had their main armament facing inland as protection from a land-based attack. By the time they were completed any threat had passed, largely due to the Franco-Prussian war of 1870, and because the technology of the guns had become obsolete.

However, there they stand to this day. And they have worked – we have never been invaded by the French since then. Indeed, one of the first things one sees as one returns to Portsmouth on a cross channel ferry is Horse Sand Fort in the Solent; the second thing we notice is *HMS Warrior* in dry dock; and the third is *HMS Victory*. Bienvenue en Angleterre, mes amis!

This then was the climate of opinion when Alfred was appointed to command *HMS Hero*[59] as part of the strategically important Channel Squadron in January 1861. He had not wasted his time between commands. In 1858, by now a Fellow of the Royal Geographical Society, he was encouraged by the Admiralty to publish the third edition of *Methods of Ascertaining the distance from Ships at Sea*. The first edition had been published in 1845 and had been deemed so important by the Admiralty that a copy was placed on every man-of-war.

Up to that point, captains couldn't be sure of hitting the target ship unless they were virtually touching it. Now, with steamers and better armaments, distances began to play a large part in actually striking a blow on an enemy warship – *HMS Warrior*, for instance, had a range of 3,800 yards. As Alfred put it….

If the reader imagines that it is safe, when firing at very distant objects, to entrust this important point to the judgment of the captains of the guns, let me ask him to try the following experiment: lay out a target at, say 1300 yards, and then ask the opinion of the officers on deck as to its distance, and note the difference in their guesses; it will be found to be very considerable.

If, under such circumstances, accuracy cannot be relied on, surely it cannot be expected, in the excitement consequent on the approach of action, when perhaps only occasional peeps at an opponent could be obtained. I dwell more strongly on this, because some officers in the service have advanced an opinion that it is a mistake to give captains of guns the elevation, saying, that they 'ought to guess at the distance'![60] Guessing at the distance may be practised as a last resource; but it cannot be prudent to trust to so vague a guide, when the means of determining it with greater accuracy are within reach. It is quite evident, therefore, that to avail ourselves fully of the expertness of our seamen, we should be able at all times to ascertain the distance from our opponent's ship. Range-boards are frequently hung up over every gun on a deck; but are we ready in the case of attack from steamers or a gun boat (the vessels most likely to choose a long range) to ascertain that which alone can render the range-board useful, viz. the distance?

Alfred, rather modestly, prefaced the book.....

I am aware that I lay myself open to the charge of presumption in writing on a subject which, it may be supposed, has attracted the attention of many officers more likely than I am to take a clear view of it.

For some time past my attention has been drawn to the subject of ascertaining the distance from ships at sea; and imagining, though perhaps vainly, that my ideas are worth communicating. I have thrown them into this shape, with the hope of making them as generally available as possible.

The book has reams of meticulously detailed tables - part of one is shown opposite. One can only marvel that they were all prepared longhand – no computers in those days! Perhaps Alfred had access to Charles Babbage's 'difference engine' the forerunner of modern computers.

And to think, these tables were to be used when the vessels were tossing in the sea, though, to be fair, Alfred understood that ...

No speed however great, no battery however heavy, no gunners however expert, no methods of ascertaining our distance from the Enemy's Ship, however accurate, will avail us if our guns are embarked in Vessels whose rapid or excessive motion prevents accuracy of practice.

So he implored his readers to use their *best means of diminishing the motion in the Ships they command.*

Alfred was fast getting a reputation as one who could examine a problem, and report on it impartially and in detail. In August 1858, Lord Salisbury, Lord President of the Council, invited him to report on the state of Navigation Schools – schools for boys between the ages of twelve

Name of the part of the Ship, Masts or Yards, on which the Observer is placed.	(C) Correction to be added to Observed Angle.	Height of the Eye above the Water, in Feet.	0° 41'	0° 40'	0° 39'	0° 38'	0° 37'	0° 36'	0° 35'	0° 34'
	' "		yds.	yds.	yds.	yds.	yds.	yds.	yds.	yds.
	4.40	20	583	598	614	631	651	672	694	716
	5.11	25	722	740	761	782	807	833	860	887
	5.43	30	864	886	910	935	964	997	1032	1062
	6.11	35	1007	1033	1060	1088	1124	1161	1204	1237
	6.40	40	1152	1183	1213	1243	1286	1329	1372	1416
	7.5	45	1296	1333	1363	1404	1444	1498	1546	1595
	7.30	50	1440	1483	1517	1564	1602	1666	1720	1734
	7.51	55	1588	1632	1671	1722	1771	1834	1894	1953
	8.12	60	1736	1782	1830	1879	1940	2002	2067	2132
	8.32	65	1882	1932	1984	2037	2106	2170	2241	2311
	8.52	70	2026	2082	2135	2195	2266	2335	2414	2490
	9.10	75	2167	2229	2285	2351	2425	2499	2587	2667
	9.28	80	2308	2367	2435	2508	2582	2663	2757	2842
	9.45	85	2452	2517	2586	2664	2741	2827	2926	3021
	10.3	90	2598	2667	2739	2819	2903	2995	3092	3200
	10.19	95	2744	2817	2889	2975	3066	3163	3265	3377
	10.35	100	2890	2967	3042	3138	3229	3330	3436	3541
	10.51	105	3035	3114	3196	3291	3392	3499	3612	3725
	11.7	110	3179	3261	3352	3444	3556	3667	3787	3907
	11.22	115	3321	3413	3500	3602	3719	3837	3955	4086
	11.38	120	3464	3565	3650	3757	3880	4001	4125	4261
	11.52	125	3607	3713	3800	3911	4038	4165	4294	4436
	12.6	130	3751	3856	3955	4065	4196	4329	4468	4610
	12.19	135	3893	4000	4109	4219	4356	4493	4639	4785
	12.33	140	4043	4149	4262	4376	4518	4661	4812	4964
	12.46	145	4189	4299	4416	4534	4682	4830	4986	5143
	13.0	150	4334	4448	4570	4693	4845	4998	5160	5323
	13.13	155	4480	4598	4724	4850	5008	5165	5334	5502
	13.27	160	4626	4747	4877	5008	5171	5334	5507	5680
	13.39	165	4772	4900	5032	5166	5334	5503	5681	5855
	13.51	170	4915	5048	5186	5324	5495	5667	5851	6030
	14.3	175	5057	5196	5336	5482	5656	5831	6020	6205
	14.15	180	5169	5339	5490	5640	5818	5994	6188	6380
	14.26	185	5342	5483	5645	5800	5979	6159	6359	6560
	14.38	190	5488	5632	5796	5960	6143	6327	6532	6738
	14.49	195	5634	5782	5950	6118	6307	6496	6706	6918
	15.1	200	5779	5931	6103	6276	6470	6664	6880	7096
	15.11	205	5926	6082	6258	6434	6633	6830	7054	7275
	15.22	210	6072	6232	6412	6593	6796	7000	7227	7454
Alteration in Distance for 1 foot in height .			yds. 28	yds. 29	yds. 30	yds. 31	yds. 32	yds. 33	yds. 34	yds. 35
Angles observed when the Vertical Method is adopted			89° 19'	89° 20'	89° 21'	89° 22'	89° 23'	89° 24'	89° 25'	89° 26'

and fifteen, who intended to make a career in the merchant navy. In his report, Alfred commented that such schools were important to generate the sort of sailors that the Royal Navy could call on in times of emergency, and important too as……

> ……the commercial marine represents England in every country, and it is desirable that our representatives should cease to exhibit (as is now frequently the case) the worst side of the national character.

Such schools had fallen into disfavour….

> ….and would soon become the last resort of those idle troublesome fellows, expelled from the agricultural class and the various trades, who are too old, too ignorant, or too profligate ever to make even indifferent sailors.

In passing, he commented on the fact that ……

> ……foreign seamen in the merchant fleet have increased in number by 262 per cent, while British seamen have only increased by 6 per cent during the last five years.

A hundred and seventy years later, and we are still dependent on foreign workers for some of the country's more menial and arduous tasks!

The report (price one shilling) was advertised in The Times adjacent to an advert for the illustrated 'Diseases of the Rectum, with Remarks on Habitual Constipation', price eight shillings. Form an orderly queue!

Later the same year, although aware that it might stand in the way of a sea command, but encouraged by his brother-in-law George Grey, Alfred accepted an appointment as one of the five commissioners – the only naval representative - on the *Royal Commission to Inquire into the Condition and Management of Lights, Buoys and Beacons on the Coast of the United Kingdom and its Colonial Possessions as compared with those on the Coasts of Foreign Countries*. They reported on 5 March 1861. The Commission had been established as a direct result of the French threat – unlike in France, the lighthouse service in Britain was not a direct department of state but comprised three authorities: the Corporation of the Elder Brethren of Trinity House (covering England, Wales and the Channel Islands), the Northern Lighthouse Board (Scotland and the Isle of Man) and the Commissioners of Irish Lights. Consequently, vast sections of the coast were not covered by lighthouses or beacons, unlike France, where lights were placed in a system where the beams would cross. Moreover, the design of British lights was relatively backward when compared with the French.

The Commission met for the first time on 19 January 1859. Their principal aim was to secure a wide range of testimony relating to the three lighthouse authorities operating in Britain. This began with the circulation of questionnaires to related practitioners including the agents of Lloyd's, prominent ship-owners, steamship companies, foreign lighthouse organisations, scientific authorities, and sailors. This questionnaire was reproduced in various newspapers, advertising the Commission's activities to a broad readership. Public interest in the activities of this governmental body reflects the close relationship between coastal periphery and urban centre in nineteenth-century Britain.

Alongside the accumulation of written evidence, the Commissioners undertook their own observations of the British lights. In the summer of 1859, the Commissioners embarked on a lengthy voyage on board the steamer *Vivid*. Boarding for the first time in Portsmouth on the 5 June 1860, they spent over a month at sea almost circumnavigating Great Britain, so as to be able to form an opinion of the efficiency of the 130 light 'establishments', of which 79 were personally inspected.

As well as commenting on the efficacy of individual stations, this tour provided evidence on a number of other concerns. The welfare of isolated lighthouse keepers, the strange phenomenon of birds colliding with lighthouse lanterns, and the necessity of installing lightning conductors on exposed towers, were all discussed in the final document.

The commissioners were indeed fortunate to be able to call on the services of the eminent scientist, Michael Faraday, whose major effort in the practical application of science was connected with lighthouses. Although the move to merge all the British lighthouse authorities was ultimately unsuccessful, Faraday played a key role in assessing the technical merits of lighthouse systems, based on detailed work he undertook at Whitby Lighthouse. He introduced French lenses and, most novel, was his close involvement with various schemes to electrify lighthouses. The scheme finally chosen was one powered by an electro-magnetic machine driven by a steam engine. Although electric lights were installed in many lighthouses, the programme was ultimately deemed a failure because of the expense involved and in 1880 it was abandoned. Despite this failure, Faraday had personally overseen one of the earliest practical applications of his invention: the electric generator, and by 1900, the entire coastline of Britain and Ireland was covered by a series of overlapping beams of light emitted by a highly engineered chain of lighthouses, beacons and lightships.

From his publications, it is obvious that Alfred's attention to detail was scientific, and he threw himself into working with such an intellect as Michael Faraday. He had first been introduced to the concept of science by his professor at the Royal Naval College, the remarkable James Inman, who had been the official astronomer on the Board of Longitude and had subsequently written *Navigation and Nautical Astronomy for Seamen*, a book that became a standard reference for all captains, and in which he devised tables to simplify the calculation of distances between two points on the surface of the earth using spherical trigonometry. In recognition of his work in nautical astronomy he was elected a Fellow of the Astronomical Society of London, forerunner of the Royal Astronomical Society.

Inman died in 1859, having planted seeds of enquiry in the mind of Alfred, and introducing him to the works of William Herschel, a giant within his field and the originator of the concept of 'deep space'. Herschel had discovered the planet Uranus in 1781, and on moving to Slough, he constructed a 40-foot telescope which was, at that time, the largest scientific instrument that had ever been built. Herschel pioneered the use of astronomical spectrophotometry as a diagnostic tool, using prisms and temperature measuring equipment to measure the wavelength distribution of stellar spectra. In addition, Herschel discovered infrared radiation. Other work included an improved determination of the rotation period of Mars, the discovery that the Martian polar caps vary seasonally, the discovery of Titania and Oberon (moons of Uranus) and Enceladus and Mimas (moons of Saturn). For any sailor, who used the stars as a map, his work was invaluable.

Corresponding with the concept of deep space was that of 'deep time', as suggested by geologist Charles Lyell, especially in his classic work of 1830 *Principles of Geology,* which used scientific evidence to reject the Biblical account of short-scale creation of the earth. It corresponded with William Herschel's concept of 'deep space' and the distance of the stars and planets. Lyell and Faraday had worked together in 1846 when they were part of a commission that examined the causes of a colliery disaster in Haswell, County Durham. Faraday had also worked closely with Humphrey Davy - so, no surprise then that Alfred revelled in the opportunity to pick his brains.

When Alfred was thirty-one, Hershel's son, John published the influential *A Discourse on the Study of Natural Philosophy* which became a hugely popular work and ran into many editions. His case was that science was based on the fundamental value of free enquiry, and that all sciences – mathematics, astronomy, optics, electricity, chemistry, magnetism, geology, botany and gases - were connected to form a single philosophy and culture.

Alfred was especially taken by Herschel's three part 'inductive method' of discovery – precise gathering of quantitive data by observation and experiment; secondly, the emergence of a general hypothesis from this data; and thirdly, the testing of the hypothesis once more by experiment and observation to see if it could be disproved. Exactly the process that Alfred employed when writing his manuals.

These scientific writings resonated powerfully with the mood of the age, but they contained potentially subversive implications for the biblical authority of Christianity. In fact, science had been chipping away at biblical orthodoxy for many years – Charles Darwin himself traced evolutionary ideas as far back as Aristotle; more recently, the thinkers of the Scottish Enlightenment asserted the importance of human reason combined with a rejection of any authority that could not be justified by reason. Darwin's grandfather Erasmus Darwin had outlined a hypothesis of transmutation of species in the 1790s, and Jean-Baptiste Lamarck published a more developed theory in 1809. Both envisaged that spontaneous generation produced simple forms of life that progressively developed greater complexity – which put paid to the notion of the immutability of species. The period between Captain Cook's expedition in the Endeavour in 1768 and Darwin's voyage to the Galapagos in the Beagle in 1831 was one of extreme scientific fertility – when Joseph Banks, William Herschel and Humphrey Davy were in their prime. Between them they created a distinctively British science and, rightly, they are still household names. Lyell, Faraday, John Herschel and Darwin were following in a rich tradition.

Nevertheless, the Church and clergy still had tremendous power in matters scientific. In particular, they held to the position of the immutability of the species, the idea that each species was created by God and did not vary over time, with each successive generation being much the same as the previous one. A challenge to this orthodoxy was considered to be not only a challenge to the scientific establishment, but also to the order of society. So, when the shy and retiring Charles Darwin reluctantly published *On the Origin of Species* in November 1859, he was only too aware of the formidable challenge he faced – for his theory of natural selection did away with the necessity of believing in a Creator and put science and religion in an opposition that remains to this day.

Despite its cost[61], the book became a best seller, and the focal point of a national debate, enhanced by a boom in publishing and media industries, along with a rapidly expanding postal service and an expanding railway network – possibly the first time that such a debate on a large scale had occurred in Britain. The most famous of such debates was held at the University Museum in Oxford in which Thomas Huxley was asked by the Bishop of Oxford, Samuel Wilberforce, whether it was through his grandmother or grandfather that he considered himself descended from a monkey. In replying, Huxley defended Darwin's theory and concluded by insisting that he was not ashamed to have a monkey as an ancestor, but that he would be ashamed to be connected to a man who used his great gifts to obscure the truth. The audience was shocked that the Bishop could be so ridiculed in public, and thus leave a legacy that it was no longer necessary to defer to senior members of the Anglican Church in matters of science.

Where did Alfred stand in this debate? As we know, he was a very keen, precise scientist, and the growing public knowledge of geology and astronomy - the recognition of 'deep space" and 'deep time' - surely meant that he could not have believed in a literal, Biblical six days of creation. But could he accept that if a new species could arise through a natural process rather than being the creation of God, was there any reason to suppose that a Creator exists at all? He was a deeply religious man from a deeply religious family - the son of a Bishop, the grandson of another Bishop, two brothers were priests, one sister was a nun – so perhaps he was content to rely on an instinctive, perhaps deliberately unexamined, belief in a benign creator somewhere, distantly, behind the great unfolding scheme of nature. He might have chosen not to try to reconcile a safe religious belief and secular materialism, being content merely to wonder at the magnificence that divine creation and science reveals. However, we may imagine that the seeds of doubt in his faith that had been planted on the premature death of his wife were fertilised, not only by Darwin, but also through his conversations with Michael Faraday. His moral convictions, though, remained fast, and he spent the rest of his life caring for those he perceived less fortunate than himself, be they members of his crew, 'fallen women', or pauper children.

Alfred took command of *HMS Hero*, a wooden screw/sail cruiser in the Channel Squadron, in January 1861. While in dock in Devonport, it was reported that

> *An able seaman named John Sanders fell out of the main chains (of HMS Hero) into the dock, a drop of about thirty feet, and was so severely injured that he died while being conveyed to the surgery.[62]*

Alfred, naturally, was concerned not only for the poor man and his family, but for his and his ship's reputation, as an accident such as this did not reflect well on them.

When the *Hero* finally left harbour on April 19, leading a squadron, she was *under topsails, topgallant sails, and royals, with jib and flying jib.* Next day she was in the *Chops of the Channel* (the southern end of the English Channel, famously hazardous to navigation) when a *16-foot shark was spotted playing under our stern!*[63], possibly a stray harmless blue shark lost as a result of a faulty navigation system.

Within a few days disaster struck. Alfred described the scene, and what was going through his mind….

> *Yesterday at about 9 o'clock in the morning – oh dear, it is really quite shocking to think what might have happened to us. I have been many years at sea and never saw anything like it before. I was standing on the Poop when an officer came and whispered in my ear 'Captain Ryder, the ship is on fire.' Now just think – a great ship all built of wood on fire, and close to the magazine full of tons of gunpowder. I had 870 men's lives to think about, besides Her Gracious Majesty's Ship Hero worth about £270,000. I should have said 869 men's lives because the Captain is always expected, and very properly, to be the last man to leave the ship and therefore is pretty sure to go to the bottom or to be blown up to the clouds.*
>
> *It would take too many sheets of paper for me to tell you all the thoughts that passed through my head. All the orders I had to give, all the various matters I had to think about. There was only one thing about which there was no doubt, that I must look and act quite collectedly as if a fire was an everyday occurrence with me. After a few moments another report came to me that the fire was increasing and the smoke very thick and dense and they could not get near the place. By this time all the 8 Fire Engines were working – and I went below, the smoke was so thick that I could not see the face of any man whom I*

touched. I could only hear their voices. The fire was in a great mass of bread contained in bags. By cutting holes in the deck over the place which was deep down in the ship under water and by deluging the place with water and by dragging the bags away, in doing which the men were nearly suffocated, we at last extinguished the fire.

We were very happy and I hope very thankful for our escape. There was a nasty smell of burned bread all the rest of the day. You can't think what a horrid thing smoke is to breath. You cry and cough and gasp and stifle and faint.[64]

Panic over and the deck repaired, the cruise continued - from about this time onwards the Navy began to stage annual cruises round the ports of the British Isles – an indication of how the French crisis had subsided. In any case, if trouble was to arise, the new electric telegraph allowed instant recall when the ships were in port, and steam power allowed them to return in almost any weather conditions. Imagine the excitement when the fleet visited a town. The shores would be thronged to watch the offshore gunnery practice, and then when they entered port….

…. the harbour for miles around teems with life, for, independent of the ships' boats gliding along from one to another vessel, or towards the shore with despatches, boats from the town and coast, plied with might and main, swarm around the leviathans, either delivering supplies or soliciting orders. Business is astir, - bakers, grocers, butchers, cabmen, ponies, bumboats, &c., are in requisition. Our post-office disgorged about 7,000 letters and papers this evening and received from on board a return supply for circulation through the length and breadth of the land. On former occasions the men of the fleet remitted by post-office orders, to their friends and families, some tens of thousands of pounds.[65]

In July, Alfred recorded *Hero's* visit to Leith….

The Edinburgh people were so pleased to see the ship. One little steamer came alongside after the other, whatever the weather was, and then their passengers wandered all over the ship, poking their noses in everywhere.

I say Edinburgh but I mean Leith – Leith is the seaport of Edinburgh which is 4 or 5 miles off. Nobody thinks of stopping at Leith who is going to see Edinburgh, it is a dirty little seaport and Edinburgh is a beautiful city – one of the most beautiful cities in the world.

Some of the old houses have 12 stories – think of 12 stories! I believe some old people never come down at all but live for years in their flats.

Later, in the same letter, Alfred sketched and described a diver who had been sent down to examine the keel of a ship that had gone aground in fog…

The diver wears a helmet and a pipe made of thick leather which goes from the boat above him to his helmet, and fresh air is forced down by a pump, so that he can stay down for some hours. These diving helmets are always used now when ships have been wrecked or when there is any building to be done under water. He looks through those bars. There is a thick piece of glass behind them. The fishes I suppose, come in and look upon him through the bars. [66]

Ten days later they anchored in the waters of Loughswilly which, because of its natural shelter and depth, was an important naval port in the north of what is now Eire.

The Londonderry Sentinel provided a graphic description of the scene….

No sight could be more beautiful. Crowds collected from many points to witness the magnificent spectacle. These seven wooden walls of old England now displayed their graceful lines, their beautiful symmetry, and gayest bunting to the admiration of hundreds, while the waters of the Lough, as if proud of their freight, reflected their spire-like masts, their thousand flags and streamers, and their stately outlines in the glassy waves beneath. Now the ships are off Dunree Fort, on which the red cross of England unfurls its folds to the wind. As each man-of-war passes a salute is fired, and in the intervals the martial strains of the well-trained bands on board each vessel are borne to the shore. The scene was of the most thrilling description, and its interest was not lessened by the fact that this exhibition of the 'pride, pomp, and circumstance' of the maritime greatness of our country was unattended by the more direful accompaniments of 'glorious war.'

As night the shores of Loughswilly were brilliantly lit up with bonfires. The glare brought out the ships into fine relief, affording a spectacle easy to be enjoyed, but difficult to describe. All the inhabitants of Buncrana likewise illuminated their dwellings, and on every side great enthusiasm was witnessed. It was most gratifying to see the cordial reception given by the people of Ennishowen to the fleet, and both officers and men feel much pleased and complimented at the reception they have met with. Perhaps in no other place since they have left Spithead have they received such a hearty welcome, and the short experience had of the members of the fleet gives reason to believe that it will be richly deserved.

Some idea may be formed of the might and majesty of England's navy, from the fact that these seven vessels carry 636 guns, with crews amounting in number to 6,250 men, being more than the entire population of Strabane. The entire horse-power is nominally 4,200 but is equal to double these figures.

> *This spectacle will produce a profound and lasting impression*
> *on the peasantry of Donegal, and the fame of it will spread*
> *throughout all the mountains and glens of the west.*[67]

Perhaps this exuberant report should be viewed in the context of the 'Irish Question', which went back to the days of Cromwell, and contained several complex and interrelated issues – religion and ethnicity, the economic structure, modes of domestic governance and the nexus between Westminster and Ireland and its various communities. All these issues had seemed to come to a head in the Great Famine of 1845-51, caused by a terrible fungal blight affecting potatoes, the staple diet of many of Ireland's rural communities. It was one of the greatest demographic catastrophes in modern history - observers reported scenes of starvation and utter misery, and the population of the west of Ireland fell by over a third.

As the famine eliminated large portions of the agrarian population, it allowed the growth of farms through mergers and acquisitions, thus enhancing the power of (English) landlords. A large number of agricultural workers emigrated, especially to the United States, Australia and England; wherever they ended up in the world, they all harboured a bitter hatred of the English. This feeling of discontent took a specific form in the establishment in Dublin in 1858 of the Irish Republican Brotherhood, or, as they were more popularly known, the Fenians, who advocated armed insurrection in Ireland and terrorism in England. They enjoyed substantial emotional and financial support from the large Irish Catholic population by this time established on the east coast of the United States, and by the mid-1860s the Fenians would boast a membership of more than 50,000, largely recruited from the lower levels of Irish agrarian society. One may only imagine their feelings when the press reported the lavish entertainment for the Channel (English) fleet when it became 'the first fleet that has ever visited the waters of Belfast' in September 1861 – the following 'dejeuner was laid out for the fleet's officers and local dignitaries (all men):

```
               BILL OF FARE.
                    SOUPS.
   Soupe Julienne                 Oyster Soup
   Puree of Fowl                  Souped Uxelles
                  ENTREES.
  Volauvent of Coxcombs        Lamb Cutlets with
      Sweetbreads                Cucumber Sauce
      Fillets of Fowl with Sauce supreme.
                 ROAST BEEF.
   Roast Turkey Poults            Roast Ducks
        Ham                        Chickens
   Oyster Crumbs                   Tongues
              Lobster Salad.
               SECOND COURSE.
   Vienna Pudding     Grouse       Meringues
 Cheese-cakes, Partridge, Preserved Ginger Puddings.
                  TRIFLES.
   Italian Creams                Lemon Creams
   Punch Jellies               Maraschino Jellies
   Puff Paste Bows               Madelines
               Apple Pie.
                 DESSERT.
   Apples         Fine Apple          Pears
   Plums          Grapes          Green Ginger
   Walnuts        Savoy Cakes       Macaroons
   French Plums   Iced Biscuit   Raisins & Almonds
 Strawberry Ice Cream        Vienelle Ice Cream
            Crystallised French Fruits.
```

After that banquet, Alfred was fortunate to be spared the Ball later that same evening.

After Belfast the Fleet moved to Dublin where Alfred *had a chat* (sic) *with the Queen, who was very gracious and asked me about the other ships. She looked very well and happy.*[68],[69]

In December Alfred and the *Hero* were sent to the North American and West Indies Station at Bermuda. A 23-year-old lieutenant, William Kennedy, wrote....

I was ordered to join the Hero, a screw line-of-battle ship of 90 guns, then lying at Spithead under sailing orders for Bermuda; so, bidding my shipmates adieu, I went straight aboard her, and an hour afterwards we were under way, the band playing "I'm off to Charlestown." Our relations with America were somewhat strained at the time, in consequence of the Mason and Slidell affair, and a large squadron was ordered to assemble at Bermuda to augment the North American Fleet under Admiral Sir Alexander Milne. Happily, the matter was peacefully arranged without bloodshed. We remained four months at Bermuda.

From Bermuda we left with the squadron for Halifax, where we had a very good time shooting and fishing and enjoying the hospitality for which that station is so celebrated, and consequently so popular with the navy; but having unfortunately run upon a sunken rock near Halifax in a dense fog, we were ordered home to pay off after a happy commission.[70]

From Halifax Alfred described a day he spent on shore....

I went to New Brunswick the other day, and up the river St John to the Grand Falls. The river is so very rapid and so shallow that they find the best kind of steam boats are those with one stern wheel – such funny looking things!

I never saw them before although I have often heard of them. The higher we get up the stream, the smaller the steam boats become and the slower they went for the stream got quicker. In some places the stream was going at 10 or 11 miles an hour and the boat could hardly stem it.

It was very cold. Winter here lasts until the middle of May.

At last we got to the Grand Falls, and very pretty they were – nothing like so grand as Niagara of course, but still very pretty.

Nearly all the fir wood we use in England comes from this pat of the world. There are a large number of men called Lumber men whose occupation is cutting down fir trees and larch and making great rafts which they float down the river to the sea, and large numbers of English ships take them home.[71]

The American Civil War had broken out in April 1861. The official British attitude was one of strict neutrality between the North and the South; there was nothing that Britain could or should do militarily to intervene in a domestic quarrel half a world away, but for good reason, political and popular opinion was deeply divided. From one perspective, the South was a quasi-aristocratic society, and as such was greatly admired by many British patricians and landowners; it was also the country's most significant supplier of raw cotton. On the other hand, the South was also a slave-owning society, and Britain had abolished slavery throughout its empire thirty years earlier. In particular, the Lancashire cotton workers were anxious when the North's blockade of the South meant they had no available cotton for them to spin.

So, neutrality was uncomfortable – and more so when in November the London bound *Trent*, a British mail steamer bearing two Confederate diplomatic envoys James Mason and John Slidell seeking to lobby for recognition of the Confederacy, was intercepted by The Union ship *U.S.S. San Jacinto* near the Bahamas. The envoys were arrested and taken back to Boston. The British were outraged when word of the interception reached London in late November; they insisted that their neutral position did not deter them from accepting any paying customer who wished to travel aboard their ships. Palmerston's government dispatched a message to the American government demanding the release of Mason and Slidell, along with an apology for the transgression of British rights on the high seas. Lincoln decided not to push the issue. On December 26, he ordered the envoys released and averted a possible war with England in the process. Such were the *somewhat strained* relations with America referred to by Lieutenant Kennedy, and into which the *Hero* was thrust as a rather underemployed patrol vessel. The only times the crew had cause to fire their guns were in training exercises. They returned to Spithead in November 1862 with 30 invalids and other civilian passengers on board, and were paid off.

Alfred immediately rushed back to Hambleden where his eighty-one-year-old mother had died in August. While at sea Alfred had managed to ensure that his mother's grave was dug in direct line of sight from her bedroom in the Cottage. He had designed her gravestone slab, so on his return he was able to oversee the placing of it. It can still be seen to this day.

Though it gave him ample time to read and write, peaceful service at sea was a dull thing for a man with Alfred's active mind. If they could not compete in lines of battle, officers could only compete through the balmy days of peace by having the most spotless, efficient ship, but the brightest holystoned decks or the most tightly coiled ropes were not where his interest lay. So, it was with some relief that, while at sea with *Hero*, Alfred was appointed to investigate discipline in the Navy and suggest reforms.

The men who manned the fleet in the 1860s were a different sort from their predecessors. Thanks to tinned meat and vegetables, their diet was improved beyond measure, pay was better (with a pension after twenty years' service), they got regular shore leave and men were no longer pressed. Nevertheless, by the middle of the century, the Admiralty realised that in order to get enough men for the fleets they would have to address the problem of flogging as a form of punishment.

The men lived under a code of discipline which sanctioned physical brutality. This ascended from the Boatswain chasing a miscreant round the deck with a knotted rope, culminating for the worst offenders in the ancient ritual of a flogging at the gangway, a ceremony attended by all the ships company and officers in full dress. The malefactor, bare backed and with a leather pad to bite on, was lashed spread-eagle to an upright grating and given between a dozen and four-dozen full weight athletic blows with a cat-o-nine-tails, which lacerated his flesh and scarred him for life – scars that a man might carry as a badge of honour! Such a flogging was more or less routine on most ships, awarded for leave breaking, drunkenness, insolence, leaving post of duty, or stealing a boat with intent to desert.

The total amount of formal corporal punishment reached a peak in 1856 with 1,397 public floggings, of which 469 were administered to boy recruits – not a statistic to encourage the recruitment of young sailors. This was the image problem that Alfred was asked to address.

Whereas politicians and local administrators in civilian life tended to be nervous of open discussion about flogging, naval officers and older seamen had no hesitation in advocating the advantages of corporal punishment for men and boys under training. Admiral Colomb, a man known for his intellect and moderation, was later to recall….

Flogging was the custom of the service, and no one minded it much. There was a certain art in being flogged which was taught on the lower deck, and a fine marine in good practice would take four dozen with a calmness of demeanour which disassociated the lash from the idea of infliction of pain by way of punishment and warning, and connected it up in people's minds with any of the ordinary and routine operations to be carried out on board ship, such as scrubbing decks.[72]

With typical thoroughness, Alfred approached his task by asking captains for their views on discipline, and subsequently produced a Table of Summary Punishments, analysed as….

First Class men to be liable to corporal punishment for certain serious offences.

All boys to be liable to corporal punishment for certain serious offences.

Boys to be punished with birch instead of the cat.

The number of offences liable to corporal punishment were reduced to eight – mutiny, desertion, repeated drunkenness, smuggling liquor, theft, repeated disobedience, desertion of place or duty and indecent conduct. 2,000 copies of his report were printed and distributed to the fleet. Within five years flogging was suspended in peacetime; it was banned in wartime in 1879.

Within days of *Hero's* crew being paid off - perhaps on the recommendations of brother-in-law Sir George Grey and his cousin Sir Frederick Grey[73], First Naval Lord, the professional head of the Royal Navy - Alfred was appointed Private Secretary to the Duke of Somerset, First Lord of the Admiralty, a position Admiral Jackie Fisher later described as….

an ideal arrangement. He has the power, he pulls the strings, he has no position, he causes no jealousy, he talks to all the Lords as their servant, and he manipulates them all and oils the machine for his special master, the First Lord, to perpetrate a job when necessary!

Little did they know it, but the predominance of British naval mastery was slowly but surely being undermined. Since this trend was to escape the attention of some navalists until well into the twentieth century, it is scarcely surprising that it was not detected by most observers at the time. These mid-century years were unprecedentedly prosperous and stable and may indeed represent the summit of the nation's global economic pre-eminence. Glad to be freed from the taxation burdens of the Crimean War and to forget the inglorious way in which it had been fought, the mid-Victorians could perhaps be forgiven for relapsing into a state of complacency about their navy – the Hampshire/ Portsmouth Telegraph noted in January 1862 that *no less than 16 vessels have been paid out of commission during the last quarter, and another 17 are likely also to be paid off on their return to England.* The paper noted that only five new warships had been commissioned during the previous three months. The irony was that because of the powerlessness of its main rivals, France, Germany and the United States, Britain's naval superiority seemed to increase while her expenditure on the fleet fell, or at least was kept steady.

While the European powers were fully occupied with the diplomatic and military struggles which accompanied the unifications of Italy and Germany, they became even less interested in those parts of the world to which Whitehall attached great importance; only the French, as ever, kept up their game of upsetting British traders in the tropics. Likewise, the British, released from Palmerstonian bluster after the great man's death[74] in 1865, were equally inclined to adopt a policy of non-intervention in Europe which, in truth, reflected the realisation that sea power alone often possessed but a limited effectiveness in the European politics of the second half of the nineteenth century.

It is true that the Navy was in a state of fast evolution, and many of the ships decommissioned were deemed unfit for modern warfare, but coordinating such a motley fleet of various ages, performance and speeds, and creating a modern battle fleet was what the First Lord (and Alfred) were expected to do – they seemed to spend most of their time during Alfred's short tenure touring steel works and inspecting the construction of ironclad ships.

Alfred was not to enjoy the life of a Whitehall mandarin for long; within six months he was promoted to Commodore and, on the strength of his support for the Royal National Lifeboat Institution (RNLI), was appointed as the curiously named Comptroller-General of the Coast Guard, based in Harwich on *HMS Pembroke*. Curiously named perhaps, but not curiously paid; his annual salary was £1,000 (about £150,000 today!) Traditionally the Coast Guard was charged with the suppression of smuggling round the coast of Britain, but by the mid-nineteenth century, with smuggling on the wane, it began to function more like an auxiliary Naval service, and importantly, as a recruitment ground for future naval personnel – by 1860 there were about 5,600 men in the service, known as 'Fleet men'. Responsibilities for revenue protection were retained, but hands-on rescue services began to be undertaken more and more by Volunteer Life Brigades and by the lifeboats of the RNLI, with the Coast Guard acting in a support role, not only acting to save lives, but also taking responsibility for wrecked vessels and the property therein.

One may imagine that Alfred's duties at the Coastguard were not too onerous, for over the next four years he found time to involve himself in several causes that he considered worthwhile – many concerning the welfare of children.

In 1866 he wrote to The Times announcing the inauguration of a scholarship for the Royal Naval Female School at Isleworth – a school established in 1840 as a boarding school for the orphaned daughters of Navy officers[75]. Two months later he wrote that the fund had raised over £100 (about £12,000 today), of which he himself had contributed £5.

Later that year he was invited to be a *commissioner appointed for the proper representation connected with all objects connected with the army, navy and navigation* in connection with the Paris Exhibition, due to be held the following year. The commissioners were chaired by Queen Victoria's second son, the twenty-two-year-old Duke of Edinburgh, a serving naval officer. The Exhibition was of sufficient importance for the South-Eastern Railway Company to announce *an additional night service to Paris, at reduced fares, and a plan for the direct transmission of large and small consignments of goods to the Exhibition by passenger train at specific through rates, including all charges for shipping, landing, entries, customs formalities and delivery at the building.*

Early in 1867 Alfred joined a group of wealthy and well-connected philanthropists who had established the Newport Market Refuge *for the object of affording nightly shelter and sustenance to the really destitute and houseless with the special view of making enquiries into their characters and of providing for the ultimate benefit of such as shall seem worthy of assistance'.* In particular they resolved *'to appropriate a portion of the funds for the establishment of a school, or otherwise providing for homeless and destitute boys who take refuge there.*

From the outset it was determined that instrumental music was to form part of the boys' training; the policy was so successful that the school became a recruitment ground for military bandsmen.[76] Alfred still maintained an involvement with the Refuge until at least 1874 for, as we will note, he had to leave the Hambleden Choir outing of that year to attend to it. Its distinguished committee included future Prime Minister W.E. Gladstone[77], who was particularly interested in the work of reclaiming prostitutes, and who patrolled at night to persuade girls to leave their life of vice. This was a cause that was to attract Alfred in his later years. He was fierce in his repudiation of so called 'fallen women'. Was this some compelling fascination? Denouncing the lure may induce the very activity it proscribes, though there is absolutely no evidence that Alfred ever strayed from the straight and narrow – his evangelical mission to help these poor souls merely reflected the views of a society unwilling to tolerate, in public, free or errant sexual ways among women. Yet his wife died when he was only thirty-five, and he spent the next thirty-three years of his life celibate.

In 1872, the Refuge reported that for the previous year....

> *4,081 nights' lodgings have been granted to men, and 4,622 to women, and 23,449 suppers, and breakfasts, consisting of ½lb. of bread and a pint of coffee have been issued.*
>
> *During the past year 95 men and 170 women have obtained employment or situations through the agency of the institution;*

and in addition to these numbers, 136 poor women, who have sought shelter in the refuge from a course of sin have been placed in penitentiaries and homes.

20 children have been put into schools to enable their mothers to go into service, and 10 others are helping to pay for the support of their babies.

Boys are sent out for upwards of an hour every day to one of the public parks, and on holidays for several hours to the public parks or Primrose Hill; they have also a spacious play-room for drill and gymnastics.[78]

A worthy cause indeed.

The welfare of merchant seamen continued to trouble navalists. Concern about the quality of the men had not abated despite measures to help them. In truth, they were recruited from the poorest sections of society, and were just not strong enough to cope with the ardours of a life at sea. Alfred's concern was that merchant seamen were the source of recruits to the Royal Navy. He had seen at first hand the desperate straits to which they were reduced after their ship had been destroyed in a wreck. He led a delegation of the Committee of the Society for the Improvement of the Condition of Merchant Seamen to discuss the issue with the President of the Board of Trade, the Duke of Richmond, in April 1867. Later that year, the Merchant Shipping Amendment Act was passed, significantly improving the lot of merchant seamen.

In June 1867 Alfred gathered with several other worthies in Lichfield, his father's old see, to establish a school for *the middle classes of England* – there were *great public schools for the wealthy, and good squires and the Government looked after the poor, so the middle classes were comparatively neglected*. They agreed that the proposed school should *be guided by the teaching of the Church of England* and should not include *Romanists*. The result was Denstone College at Uttoxeter, which began life in 1873 as part of the Woodard Foundation, the flagship independent boarding school of the midlands with 46 boarding boys as pupils. Today the school still flourishes as an independent boarding school, with 620 pupils of both sexes.

In 1864 Alfred had been honoured to be appointed one of eleven naval aide-de-camps to the Queen. Though the position was largely ceremonial, he was required to attend state functions – such as the State Ball at Buckingham Palace (with 1,700 other guests) in May 1865. Stamina was required, as, like most state entertainments, the festivities didn't begin till 10pm! He had to relinquish the appointment when he was promoted to the rank of Rear-Admiral in April 1866.

Admiral Sir Alfred Ryder

Hambleden Cottage by sister Harriet Amelia

In the library of the Cottage. Alfred standing to the left.

Storming Serapaqui

Alfred as a Captain - note the curls!

The Harbour of Balaclava, 26th December 1854

Alfred Ryder

BALACLAVA

Alfred's sketch of Balaclava harbour 26 December 1854

HMS Dauntless in rough water, imagined by Alfred

Louisa, Alfred & Eddy

Picnic on McNab's Island, Nova Scotia 1862 Sketched by Alfred

Alfred with Eddy

V

HMS Bellerophon & HMS Minotaur 1868 Painted by Alfred

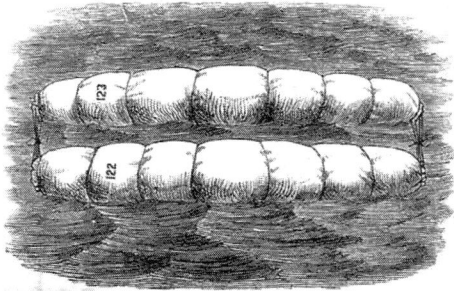

REAR-ADMIRAL RYDER'S FLOATING HAMMOCKS FOR SAVING LIFE AT SEA.

How to use your hammock as a lifebelt - designed by Alfred

HMS Audacious, Alfred's Flagship on the China Station

Eddy in the year that he died

St Mary's Hambleden, before restorations

Wellswood, Torquay

THE LATE ADMIRAL SIR ALFRED P. RYDER K.C.B.

Alfred in the uniform
of an Admiral, similar
to the one in which he
drowned in

7

Somewhere, Across the Sea

How shall we sing the Lord's song in a strange land?

Psalm 137:4

In the decade and a half after the death of Lord Palmerston in 1865, British politics revolved around the rivalry of the brilliant and dramatic Benjamin Disraeli and the intensely devout and earnest William Ewart Gladstone, the leaders of the Conservative and Liberal parties respectively. They were both faced with the same dilemma – to balance demands for reductions in the military estimates without compromising national and imperial security. Successive governments became increasingly inclined to adopt a policy of non-intervention in Europe – a tradition which was later to be given the proud, though rather misleading, name of 'splendid isolation' – induced by an awareness that Britain did not possess the armed forces necessary to intervene on the continent with any prospect of success. With an army the size of Switzerland's, and which was to a large extent locked up in India, Britain's ability to influence continental affairs through military pressure was negligible.

The army was useful, though, in quelling insurrections in distant lands. For example, in 1866, a group of British subjects had been imprisoned by the Emperor of Abyssinia. Prime Minister Disraeli issued an invasion order to the Governor of Bombay, for that is where the necessary troops were stationed. Within a few months the invasion force set sail from Bombay to the Red Sea. On board the flotilla were 13,000 British and Indian soldiers, 26,000 camp followers, 13,000 mules and ponies, an equal number of sheep, 7,000 camels, 7,000 bullocks and 1,000 donkeys – not to mention 44 elephants. After a three-month slow and inexorable slog over mountains and through deserts, and with the band playing 'Garry Owen', it took just two hours to kill more than 700 insurgents and wound 1,200 more[79]. Only twenty British soldiers were injured; none killed. All that was required of the Navy was to transport the army.

This period has been described as the 'Dark Ages of the Victorian Navy' - Britain was at peace (at least in Europe) and the Navy was required to do little more than *redress grievances, maintain the peace, combat piracy, avenge outrage and prevent disorder among shippers of guano*[80]. The problem for the Navy was that this role as the world's policeman occurred against a backdrop of unprecedented economic and technological change. The introduction of new technologies meant that expensive new battleships became obsolete almost before they were completed, though sails were still necessary for warships cruising distant seas where coaling stations were few and far between. New technology meant new tactics - there could never be certainty again.

Perhaps unsurprisingly, the strategy employed by the Admiralty was confused and muddled. The navy was in danger of being undermanned and out-matched by her greatest rivals until Hugh Childers, First Lord of the Admiralty, 1868-71, reorganized a chaotic administration. But, in fact, despite budget restraints, the Royal Navy remained supreme in the world. The building of ironclads combined with the preoccupation of the United States with post civil war reconstruction after 1865, and the decline of the French fleet after the Franco-Prussian War, meant that it was difficult for other nations to challenge British naval supremacy. However, it was unmistakeable that industrial technology and invention had taken over from fighting men and sailors, and that the effectiveness of sea power itself and the predominance of British naval mastery in particular, was being slowly but surely undermined, not least by an emerging Germany.

In such a climate, one in which officers had little to do but keep their ships spick and span, Alfred was promoted as second in command of his old fleet – the Channel Squadron. *A distinguished and meritorious officer, well deserving of his promotion* was how it was reported[81]. Again, time was spent on a goodwill tour of Britain. When the Squadron moored in the Clyde…

…the good people of the West of Scotland vied with each other in proffering a healthy welcome, and such hospitality as wealth and refined taste could display for the officers of the Channel Squadron[82].

In June he wrote from *HMS Bellerophon* what was to be his last letter to Eddy. It includes an insight into the confused mindset of the Admiralty. He wrote that….

We pass our time in exercising Steam Evolution, Exercising the sailors aloft, Exercising them at the guns, at small arms etc.

It seems his life was not too urgent ….

I have a dinner party every day at 7 o'clock for 8, 10 or 12 persons – read, chat, visit the deck occasionally until 1, after midnight then throw myself on my cot half dressed. The Flag Lieut calls me at daylight about 3 to tell me whether my three children the Bellerophon, the beautiful Achilles and the Defence are at proper distances from the Minotaur (the flagship), & from one another. If they are not, I have to chide them, and insinuate to them that although they may "try to be good boys they don't succeed" but are "lamentable failures"!!!. Having told them what signals to make I turn around for another nap. At 6.30 he calls me again with fresh news of "my family".

At 7 my bath is ready. At 7.30 I go on deck & walk the bridge until ¼ to 9 when I go to breakfast. Prayers at 9. We lunch at 1 o'clock. During the day at odd times I read some professional work or write paragraphs for my report on the Bellerophon, and on the fleet of the future as I think it should be built.

The band plays beautifully at my breakfast time its brass instruments. At my dinner time it plays string instruments.[83]

A rather boring life, perhaps, for an officer who craved action and intellectual stimulation, but not, I suspect, for Alfred, who as he intimated, had plenty of time for his reading and writing. Nonetheless, he complained, ominously, that….

> *I am on deck most of the day and must get a new backbone when I return to England, as this is worn out.*

This is not to say that Alfred did not revel in a strong gale and a good sail. From Malta in January 1857, after a prolonged period in harbour, he wrote…

> *Papa wants to have his hat put on and tied under his chin, and his thick boots put on – and go away for a run.*[84]

From the Chops of the Channel….

> *Why do you think it is called the Chops of the Channel? Because it blows so hard here. We have got a very nice little gale – obliging us to have three reefs in our Topsails, and one reef in the Courses. I wish you could see the fleet. It looks so pretty.*[85]

But gales were not without hazards….

> *We have had such a gale. I never saw it blow harder. Nearly all my sails, although some of hem were nearly new, blew right away and if I had not fortunately got the steam up, the heavy seas would have washed right over us. As it was, our Main Yard, that great piece wood that looks so strong as if nothing could break it, snapped like a carrot, and I was very glad to steam into a very safe harbour called Blacksod Bay (North County Mayo, Ireland). Two of my ships were so injured in the gale that they were ordered home to England for repair.*[86]

For a serious naval strategist, Alfred was surprisingly ambivalent about Bellerophon (or Billy Ruffian, as he called her[87]) and ironclads in general. He wrote nostalgically….

> *That we should throw away those iron plates………. We should trust to sails and pop guns as we did before when we won our glorious victories.*[88]

However, he had to face reality – iron plated steam ships were now the primary naval warships, and his ship, the *Bellerophon* was state of the art. She had been designed to resolve the problems that had become apparent in *HMS Warrior* – both had a full sail plan and a powerful steam engine, but *Bellerophon*, although she looked like the prototype British ironclad, was shorter, perhaps stubbier. The new ship marked the end of the full-length broadside. *Bellerophon* had fewer guns, but they were much heavier and concentrated amidships in an armoured battery. She performed better than *Warrior* at sea due to her reduced size, and she had thicker armour. She was a link in a rapid process of evolution that saw innovative ships rendered obsolete soon after they dazzled the world. By 1876 she was outdated.

The goal of ship designers in the later 1860s was to place extremely heavy guns in armoured gun turrets. Several experimental designs were tried, one such being *HMS Captain*, a revolutionary ship, born amid much controversy. She was built in deference to public opinion expressed in Parliament and in the press – even the Prince Consort was said to be in favour of it - but contrary to the express views and opinions of the Admiralty. Such was the clamour to put her through her sea trials, that she was launched before her buoyancy tests were complete. Six months after launch, in September 1870, she was off Cape Finisterre in what were described as *rather unexceptional wind conditions* when waves began crashing over her. Her upper deck was not far above the waves at the best of times, but now they engulfed the vessel. Her towering masts and rigging did not help in these conditions; they added to the ship's instability. She began to heel dangerously to starboard. The roll increased and just after midnight she capsized. Just eighteen men survived; 480[89] perished in the stormy waters, including the sons of the First Lord of the Admiralty, Hugh Childers, and Under-Secretary of State for War[90], Thomas Baring............and fifteen-year-old Midshipman Edward Ryder, Alfred's nephew, son of brother Spencer who was serving in India at the time. Alfred led the family mourning – he had been instrumental in arranging for the boy to enter the Navy. Prayers were offered in Hambleden, and Alfred arranged for a stained-glass window to be dedicated to Edward's memory in St Anne's Church, Portsmouth, the spiritual home of the Royal Navy. The adjacent plaque reads:

IN MEMORY OF
CHARLES DUDLEY RYDER
SON OF HON. HENRY RYDER BISHOP
OF LICHFIELD & COVENTRY. MIDSHIPMAN
OF HMS NAIAD WHO WAS DROWNED
ON MAY 28 1825 OFF CIVITA VECCHIA
ALSO OF
EDWARD DUDLEY RYDER
SON OF LIEUT COL SPENCER CD RYDER
MIDSHIPMAN OF HMS CAPTAIN WHO
WAS DROWNED WHEN THAT VESSEL
FOUNDERED ON SEPTEMBER 7 1870
OFF CAPE FINNISTERRE. THIS
WINDOW IS PLACED HERE BY ADMIRAL
ALFD P RYDER BROTHER OF CHARLES
& UNCLE OF EDWARD DUDLEY RYDER

(After his death, a memorial to Alfred himself was added to an adjacent window by *Brother officers and members of the Naval Church Society.*)

Fortuitously, Alfred was already in Hambleden, as he had been granted six weeks sick leave to seek a remedy for the pains in his back. During his time there he was elected to the committee of the new Henley Nursing Home. It was reported that *'the nurses are to be employed in the town and the neighbourhood for the poor, and also for others, each person to pay according to their means.'* On the same page as the article on the nursing home, the Henley Standard carried a report of an accident that is worth repeating in full….

As a horse drawing an empty coal truck was passing the shop
of Mr Theobald of Bell Street, grocer, on Monday morning last,
it suddenly reared and plunged its fore-feet and head through

the shop window, breaking six panes of glass together with the sash frame and sundry bottles of pickles etc, the contents of the shelves. The horse was much cut about the head and chest. Mr Mellett, veterinary surgeon, attended the animal at its stable, and whilst sewing up the wounds, received so severe a kick from the animal that he was obliged to be conveyed home.

No mention as to the state of the poor nag!

After his recuperation, Alfred travelled to Paris in his new position as Naval Attaché - he spoke French[91] and had been involved in the 1867 Paris Exhibition. The British government was beginning to realise that any European threat was unlikely to come from France; it was much more likely to come from Prussia whose power had been increasing inexorably since Otto von Bismarck was appointed Chancellor in 1862. Bismarck favoured a 'blood-and-iron' policy to create a united Germany under the leadership of Prussia. He engineered short, decisive wars with Denmark and Austria over Schleswig Holstein.[92] By 1870 all Germanic states except the pro-French, southern kingdoms of Bavaria, Baden and Württemberg were united as the North German Confederation.

Then it was only a matter of time before Bismarck seized the opportunity to wage war with France in order to draw the independent southern German state into an alliance with the North German Confederation. The war started in July 1870; within six months, it was all over. Britain played no direct part in the war beyond securing from both participants a commitment to respect Belgium's neutrality in line with the 1839 Treaty of London – the very treaty that forty-four years later would tip Britain into the Great War. Britain's limited military resources ruled out any armed intervention, and Gladstone's Cabinet could only look on as Bismarck annexed the French provinces of Alsace and Lorraine. Nor was Britain able to take effective action when in October 1870, Russia began naval manoeuvres in the Black Sea, much to the irritation of old Crimean hands like Alfred.

As an observer, a collector of intelligence, Alfred was able to report back to the Admiralty on the extraordinary success displayed by

Bismarck's troops, especially the role played by the railway. Bismarck had been able to mobilise over a million men within eighteen days, and 462,000 were transported to the French frontier in the same time – a triumph of superior preparation. Alfred could see that with the advent of rail, the competitive advantage of having the most powerful navy in the world was being eroded. A land power could be freed from its dependence on the sea – the transport of goods and men which had for centuries been cheaper and faster by water, now became easier by land. The traditional British strategy in European conflicts of dispatching expeditions would now be a much riskier proposition if the enemy could swiftly rush a far greater force to a threatened point by rail instead of having to rely upon road communications and forced marches. A land power was now freed from its dependence on the sea.

Alfred was marooned in Paris as the Germans overran northern France, and laid siege to the city during the winter of 1870, one of the coldest on record. Conditions were awful. Due to a severe shortage of food, Parisians were forced to slaughter whatever animals were at hand. Rats, dogs, cats, and horses were the first to be slaughtered and became regular fare on restaurant menus. Once the supply of those animals ran low, the citizens of Paris turned on the zoo animals residing at Jardin des Plantes. Even Castor and Pollux, the only pair of elephants in Paris, were slaughtered for their meat, and tronc au vin became quite fashionable, along with brochettes de foie de chien à la maître d'hôtel.

The sheer scale of the German victory over France – a victory most contemporaries had not predicted – traumatised the French, and led to a lasting enmity between France and Germany. After 1871, France was bound to seek every opportunity to contain a new and formidable power on its eastern border, and Germany believed its army was impregnable on the continent of Europe. It is hard to overstate the world-historical impact of this new order. Relations between the European states would henceforth be driven by a new and unfamiliar dynamic, directly leading to the events of 1914.

Someone who saw the awful potential of the new power of Germany was Benjamin Disraeli who even before the war had ended, told the House of Commons that…….

> *The war represents the German revolution, a greater political event than the French Revolution. There was not a single diplomatic tradition that has not been swept away. The balance of power has been entirely destroyed, and the country which suffers more and feels the effects of this change most, is England.*

What he was referring to was not the rise of Germany per se, but the untethering of Britain's old enemy, Russia, from the settlement imposed on her after Crimea. The purpose of the Crimean peace treaty had been to restrict the Russian navy, and so prevent Russia from threatening the eastern Mediterranean and disrupting British land and sea routes to India[93]. But after their 1871 defeat, the French renounced their opposition to Russian militarisation and sought an alliance with her to oppose any further German threat. It was Russia, not Germany, that Disraeli and successive prime ministers somewhat short-sightedly saw as posing the most significant long-term threat to British interests.

What perhaps terrified the British establishment more than the potential threat from Russia or Germany was what happened in Paris in the months following the war. A hotbed of working-class radicalism and anarchists, Paris was primarily defended during this time by the often politicised and radical troops of the National Guard rather than regular Army troops, and a Commune was established to govern the city. On 18 March, soldiers of the Commune's National Guard killed two French army generals, and the Commune refused to accept the authority of the French government. The Commune governed Paris for two months, until it was suppressed by the regular French Army during 'La semaine sanglante' (The Bloody Week) beginning on 21 May 1871. Although the Commune did not last long, Britons wondered uneasily whether the same thing could happen in their country. It seems improbable that the events could not have made an indelible impression on Alfred.

Returning to England in 1871, he took some time off to be with Edward – the census of that year shows them both staying with his old Channel Fleet friend, Captain Field and his wife at their home in Alverstoke, Hampshire. While there, with the demise of *HMS Captain* in mind, he wrote a learned paper on the '*Form of Registering Rolling Motion at Sea*' which he presented to the Social Sciences Association, to some acclaim. Also, with the *Captain* in mind, and particularly in memory of his own nephew, Alfred was one of a committee that raised over £400 for a brass memorial for those that had perished to be raised on a wall in St Paul's Cathedral. It can be seen to this day. In a letter to the Times he absolved the officers and crew of any culpability. He wrote….

> There can be no doubt – the country, acting through a public department, the Admiralty, placed 500 public servants in an unseaworthy vessel which capsized in a **summer gale**. (original emphasis) So unsuspicious was this public department of the unseaworthiness of the Captain, that neither Sir Thomas Symonds nor Sir Alexander Milne, the Admirals, received any the slightest caution as to the dangerous nature of the vessel placed under their orders.[94]

Perhaps prompted by this tragedy, he submitted a report on the lifesaving qualities of mattresses stuffed with granulated cork to the Admiralty early in 1872, so continuing the theme of sailors' welfare that ran through his life….

> It is well known that the boats of a man-of-war are, as a general rule, insufficient in number and capacity to save her crew except in the calmest of water; also, that the largest and safest are stowed on the booms, from whence time is required to move them to the water – probably not less than ten minutes at sea in the daytime in fine weather – and, of course, in other circumstances, a much longer time.[95]

His ingenious solution, to provide some temporary relief at least, was for the Navy to substitute cork-filled mattresses for the current hair mattresses that have no permanent buoyancy. With typical Victorian prudence, he suggested that cork mattresses would be a considerable advantage, not only on account of their great buoyancy, but also owing to their *economy of cost*. With his usual scientific approach, he had proved that ….

> …. six men, if they are self-possessed and have been exercised in 'hammock-floating drill' could be supported by two hammocks lashed together, and if the hammock was made of modern closely woven cotton canvas rather than the traditional coarse hempen material it would stay afloat longer. Furthermore, now that the cork is granulated by machinery, and with rib pieces inserted to prevent the cork moving, the mattresses are found quite comfortable to sleep on. In conclusion, the lives of British men-of-war seamen are very valuable. But if the question of expense is raised, it is observed that at present cork is not half the price of horsehair mattresses.[96]

Sadly, this was too revolutionary for the old guard, and was not adopted; sailors continued to drown.

The education and training of officers was a subject that exercised the Navy, and Alfred in particular. As a cadet, he had been fortunate to be a member of one of the last intakes at the Royal Naval College in Portsmouth, but that had closed in 1837, after which all youngsters setting out on a naval career proceeded directly to sea. As well as literally learning the ropes, the boys had formal lessons on board – normally taught by the Chaplain, of whom Alfred was despairing. He, unusually unsympathetically, complained that they were ignorant *of the purpose of a sextant, had never seen a chart, and had never seen a theodolite*. Unsurprising – they were Chaplains, after all! He did, however acknowledge that things were getting better with the 'experiment' of the *Britannia* – a wooden hulk that had been laid down before the Battle of Waterloo, and after active service had become a hospital ship at Portsmouth, and then in 1859, a cadet training ship. She was moved to Portland in 1862 and then Dartmouth in 1863, where she served as residential barracks for cadets. Over the next forty years *Britannia* was replaced by other hulks, until finally being replaced by buildings. Dartmouth continues to this day as the naval academy of the United Kingdom, and the officer training centre of the Royal Navy; it is now known as *HMS Dartmouth, Britannia Royal Naval College.*

Notwithstanding that they had done away with all formal training for over twenty years, the Admiralty were unhappy with progress in initial officer training. Alfred's evidence to the 1874 Rice Committee on the problem was important for as well as being a naval captain he had been Private Secretary to Edward Seymour, First Lord, so not only did he have experience of policy relating to young officer training but also access to official statistics. He was concerned with the wastage – the number of cadets and midshipmen who failed to graduate to lieutenant due to voluntary release or discharge for misconduct. In a debate at the Royal United Services Institution in 1872, he suggested that the problem was due to the policy of indiscriminate entry.

With typical Victorian prudence, he was keen to secure the best return on the outlay of public money. He was bitterly critical of the nomination system which made begging and interceding necessary to get a boy's name onto the list of naval recruits. He maintained this system only produced *'success only for those parents whose politics were of the same colour as those of the political party in power, and which often resulted in the Navy receiving the fool of the family'*. He argued that *'indiscriminate competition among boys of only 13 years old, chosen from all sections of the community was a move that would prove most mischievous'*. What was required, he argued, was not more competition, but less; dedicated naval streams should be established in designated public schools that would *'bring to the surface exactly the description of the raw material we want'*. The candidates produced would be superior to the present entry, not because of their educational accomplishments, but rather because they would demonstrate the *polished manners, high principles and firm tone of character that every intelligent English gentleman admires* – in other words, like him! He argued that in the face of looming indiscriminate entry, his plan would guarantee the only safe compromise.

He favoured special schools like Eastman's Royal Naval Academy, originally in Southsea and later at Winchester. Between 1855 and 1923 it was known primarily as a school that prepared boys for entry to the Royal Navy. He would have approved of the founding of the Nautical College, Pangbourne in 1917, the purpose of which was to prepare boys to become officers in the Merchant Navy.

When presenting the prizes to cadets of *HMS Worcester*[97] in 1878, he noted that no doubt they were all very comfortable on the *Worcester*, but when they went to sea, they must be prepared to rough it a good deal more. Any boy worth his salt would call that fun. He recounted how he had gone to sea when he was only thirteen years old, and had had to rough it a good deal, but he looked back on those days as having been the best of fun. To cheers all round, he declared that in his opinion a lad who naturally took to the sea and fitted himself for it would lead one of the happiest lives possible.

Be that as it may, whereas the Navy in the long lee of Trafalgar longed for another decisive victory, it was not developing the individuals who would be able to take the lead in such a battle. The education of officers, recruited almost exclusively from the middle class and the public schools, did not foster the initiative and the freedom of thought under pressure that Nelson had instilled in his senior officers. None of the heroes of Trafalgar – Nelson, Collingwood, Hardy – were public school educated. In fact, they all came from relatively humble backgrounds, and had educations to match. But Nelson knew that nothing is sure in a sea battle, so he left his captains free from hampering rules by telling them that *No captain can do very wrong if he places his ship alongside that of the enemy.* In short, circumstances would dictate the execution of the engagement. Nelson's famous flag hoist opening Trafalgar was the last he made during the battle – not because of his death, but because he needed no other. By contrast, when called on to deliver a naval showdown in the Great War, the Navy found that its officers were too bound by rigidity of thought and subservience to higher authority to demonstrate the required enterprise. Captains waited upon the orders of their admiral, and if these were lacking or confused – as Admiral Beatty's often were – subordinates never dared to think for themselves. An atmosphere of oppressive masculinity suggested a floating boarding school, and even prefects (ships' captains) were fearful of adopting any course of action without their headmaster's consent. The sudden exercise of tactical initiative would have been an unnatural rejection of the culture that had nurtured them through their entire professional lives – a culture that would inevitably lead to misunderstandings and missed opportunities, not least at Jutland in 1916.

Alfred's next appointment was as Naval Attaché to the curiously named Maritime Courts of Europe. Free-trade, industrialisation and rising prosperity had made Britain the centre of world trade, dependent as no other country was upon the import and export of commodities. The coming of the steamship and refrigeration permitted foreign farmers to take advantage of the lack of tariffs and to flood the British market with their products. Thousands of merchant ships criss-crossed the world. Although most were bound for Britain, the burgeoning continental markets, not least the newly unified states of Germany and Italy, were also becoming significant markets. A newly unified country across the Atlantic was also beginning to flex its mercantile muscles. It was of vital importance, therefore, that not only was the law of the sea maintained by the Royal Navy, but that there was also some commonality in maritime civil law – the arrangements that governed marine commerce, marine navigation, salvage, maritime pollution, seafarers' rights, and the carriage by sea of both passengers and goods.

The Admiralty, naturally, sought to be the international arbiter of maritime law, but other countries had different ideas, and it was the exchange of intelligence throughout Europe that exercised Alfred. It was, perhaps, a strange appointment for someone with no legal training, but he was something of a linguist[98], was prepared to travel (he journeyed through Russia, Italy and Austria) and was a man who could be relied on – an experienced and trusted, safe pair of hands – and for which he was paid £500 a year in addition to half his naval pay, plus £1 a day subsistence expenses.

Back in London, in May 1873 he presented a paper to the Royal United Services Institution on the necessity for good ventilation on ships, especially in hospital ships. He presented detailed drawings of how a ship should expel foul air while allowing in fresh air (which he referred to as the 'plenum'), employing ice-making machines in the tropics, and the placing of stoves for colder latitudes.

> *For my own part, I believe the true principle of ventilating ships as well as buildings is the principle of exhaustion, and you will really do very little good unless you thoroughly and completely adopt the system of getting rid of the foul air, by artificial means, if you please, and leaving the supply of pure and fresh air to natural means, which will be easily accomplished.* [99]

He showed that the most important part of the ship to preserve clean air was the hold, and he had in all the ships he commanded adopted a plan which consisted of separating the contents of the hold in two parts, so as to have a passage through the centre, and thus to secure ventilation.

Seems so obvious to us today, but experimental in 1873.

After rumours that he was to be made Commander in Chief of the North America and West Indies Station, in 1874 Alfred, now a Vice-Admiral, was appointed to command the China Station – an area of thousands of square miles of ocean, thousands of miles of coastlines, thousands of miles of rivers, and thousands of British citizens to protect.[100] His brief was simple(!) – to keep the coasts, seas and rivers free from pirates so that trade may not be impeded; to increase Britain's influence in what she regarded as part of her informal empire through diplomacy, and if necessary, by force; to continue Palmerston's 1850 edict that every *British subject, in whatever land he may be, shall feel confident that the watchful eye and the strong arm of England, will protect him against injustice and wrong;* and to keep an eye on Russia. To do this he was given a fleet of 21 ships, 2,000 officers and men and 112 guns.

Hambleden Parish Magazine reported his appointment with mixed feelings, but with a sense of reflected pride in his important command....

> *We are both glad and sorry to learn that our kind friend Vice Admiral AP Ryder has been appointed to the command of the China Station. We are glad for this honour done to one who*

so richly deserves it, and for the good which he will hereby be enabled to do, and sorry for our own loss of his presence for three years.[101]

How would a Victorian have viewed China and the Far East? By any measure, China and Great Britain were two of the great powers in the mid nineteenth century. China's largest domestic product, which some saw as its most sinister export, was its people: cheap, docile, even servile labour. Alfred would have come across Chinese wharfingers in the docks of Britain as many Chinese seamen, it was suspected, jumped ship in England. 'Chinatowns' were established in London's Limehouse, and in Liverpool, Cardiff and Bristol. These communities were predominantly male and were viewed with suspicion - legends arose about the diseased, promiscuous, hypnotic oriental, who ate cats and rats, gambled inveterately and was addicted to opium. Their laundries - chief on-shore Chinese employment - were commonly assumed to be mere facades for unspeakable vices; in any event, they deprived poor white working-class women of an important source of supplementary income.

So, In the absence of any extensive contacts with China, the English constructed their own images of the country and its people from a hazy knowledge of history, from cultural impressions, and from philosophical preconceptions. They weren't about to let ignorance stand in the way of expressing an opinion! Favourable opinions were represented mostly by the fashions for Chinese landscapes and architecture, for Chinese horticulture (clematis and rhododendron), for China tea (though overtaken by India and Ceylon), and for Chinese porcelain, silks and furniture. That China had once led in science and technology, inventing paper, printing, gunpowder, cannons, compasses, and so forth, was well known, but there the wholehearted appreciation ended.

Attempts were made to provide insight into Chinese culture by Coleridge with his 1816 poem *Kubla Khan*, and the photographs of John Thomson whose photography in the late 1860's of the Far East enlightened the Victorian audience about the land, people, and way of life of China and South-East Asia. Although Chinese ceramics had been promoted in

Britain from the early 1870's, unlike their Japanese counterparts, they barely caught on. The V&A acquired its first group of Chinese objects in 1852 and a handbook was published, but it was peppered with dismissive comments about the Chinese character....

> *It would hardly be supposed that an effeminate race such as the Chinese would have a taste for working in metal. But it should be remembered that they have not always been a degenerate race softened by luxury and by too great a facility for enjoyment.*

Travellers, diplomats and traders returning to Britain reported that the mass of the Chinese was illiterate. Study and writing were confined to a mandarin civil service, entry to which was judged by the same examination set for over a millennium. Here, surely, was a society which had somehow got stuck, indeed perhaps deliberately maimed itself. The symbol of the Chinese lady's compressed foot and the long, uncut talons of fingernails worn by the nobility exercised a powerful hold upon the British as they wrestled with the riddle of China's arrested development.

They reasoned that the causes of China's stagnation seemed not hard to find. The absurdly archaic language impeded communication and condemned the masses to social immobility; the degenerate religions licensed superstition and prohibited rigorous philosophical inquiry; the effete central government provoked wasteful civil wars; the parasitic nobility enthroned punctiliousness and lethargy; and the corrupt bureaucracy institutionalized evasiveness and torpor. The people themselves were sunk in the stupidity of sterile ancestor-worship and unremitting manual toil or else prone to orgies of cruelty, fits of gambling and drug-induced reveries.

However, the desire to reach this alien, but enormous and virtually unexploited market drove hundreds of British traders to China in the early nineteenth century – the famous trading company Jardine, Matheson[102] & Co was established in Canton (modern Guangzhou) in 1832, trafficking opium while trading cotton, tea, silk and a variety of other goods. The Jardines and Mathesons made huge wealth from their trading activities, but that did not mean they held the Chinese in any regard. In 1836, James Matheson described them as *a people characterised by a marvellous degree of imbecility, avarice, greed and obstinacy,* and reasoned it *was unjust that the Chinese should possess a vast portion of the most desirable parts of the earth* when they were not willing to share their wealth with foreigners.

Nevertheless, by the mid-century British trade with China was well established, but activities were severely restricted by the Chinese authorities. Tea was exported in enormous quantities, along with silk, lacquer and porcelain, but China showed no interest in buying goods from the West. Not only did the Chinese not want traded goods, the Chinese Emperor and the scholarly officials were as contemptuous and dismissive of the British as the British were of them. The Chinese regarded commerce as a *well-known barbarian idiosyncrasy,* and a merchant was a totally contemptible figure. They simply did want the British there.

Britain sought to redress this trade imbalance by selling the manufactured goods that were being produced in such abundance in Britain, together with two products from British India: raw cotton and opium[103].

The trade in opium[104] was illegal, but extremely profitable – to the British, though not, one may imagine, to the Chinese. The devastating effects of drug addiction and the damage it did to the economy and the health of its people were of grave concern to the Chinese imperial court. Such concerns were shrugged off by the British authorities; they could not allow anything to interrupt the trade, and so, in 1839, when 20,000 cases of opium (1,200 tons) were seized by Chinese officials, they needed no further excuse to send warships to attack Canton. China was not prepared for a war with a western power and was easily defeated in what became known as the First Opium War. By the terms of the 1842 Treaty of Nanking, China was forced to open five so-called treaty ports[105] to foreign residents, trade and consular establishments. It also had to cede Hong Kong in perpetuity to the British. Treaties with other foreign powers soon followed and the number of foreigners on Chinese soil began to grow, with merchants in particular continually pressing for greater access to Chinese markets. Problems again erupted, and by 1857 China and Britain were at war once more, with the same result - more treaty ports were opened and, more significantly, Britain was granted the right of an ambassador in Peking. A third round of hostilities broke out in 1860, during which British and French troops marched on Peking, and amid bouts of looting, torched the Imperial Summer Palace. Again, the Chinese capitulated.

Some saw this as a seminal moment that marked yet another chapter in the triumph of the west....

> *Thus, it has been the destiny of England, ran one report in the British press, to break down a government fabric which has so long mystified the European world, and to uncover to its own subjects its hollowness and its evils.*

And....

> *The mysterious and exclusive barbarism of the Chinese Empire had been dismantled by the force of active intrusive Western Civilisation.*[106]

This was the China that greeted(!) Alfred – a suspicious, humiliated, and seeming backward country, reluctant to embrace western civilisation, and whose culture was generally disregarded. Although Chinese goods continued to be imported into Britain in the nineteenth century, it was Japanese objects that took the country by storm - no middle-class drawing room was without its Japanese fan or teapot; Japan was held up to be the antithesis of China. Up to 1853 Japan was just as mysterious as China; it had maintained a closed-country policy for over two hundred years, but in that year an American naval squadron arrived demanding that the country open its ports to foreign powers. Japan did not welcome western intrusion with open arms, but was aware of what had happened in China and realised it had no chance against superior forces.

As with China, the western image of Japan was also partly formed through photography. The images and accompanying commentaries of the Anglo-Italian photographer, Felix Beato helped to create what became the dominant image of Japan - as simple, rustic and picturesque. Both China and Japan were compared to the Middle Ages, but whereas with

China it was the backwardness of an era long gone that was envisaged, with Japan it was the romance of something only recently lost that appealed – a fanciful image reinforced by Gilbert and Sullivan with *The Mikado*, first performed in 1885, and which remains the most frequently performed Savoy Opera.

The rosy tinted vision of Japan changed after the revolution of 1868. The new Japanese government, fearful of the same imperialist pressures that they observed happening in nearby China, adopted the slogan 'Enrich the country, strengthen the army' and sought to create a nation-state capable of standing equal among Western powers. They turned to Britain and other European nations for help. British engineers constructed lighthouses and railways; British shipbuilders and naval architects helped build up Japan's commercial and naval fleets; and British instructors taught English, mathematics and physics. In fact, Alfred himself would host three Japanese sea cadets on *Audacious* in 1879 in a course of 'practical instruction.' So, by the time Alfred assumed command of the China Station Japan was well on the way to realising its political ambitions – a country not only capable of defending itself against foreign incursions but also increasingly able to join the imperial scramble for territory itself.

The fourth strand of Alfred's tasks was provided by Russia. Britain regarded China as part of its informal empire; in terms of its trade potential, it was infinitely more important to Britain than Africa, and Alfred's chief task was to protect that position – in particular, from an ambitious Russia. Russia's ambitions in Asia were motivated in part by the need to expunge its humiliation in the Crimea, but mainly by the fear that the British would engross the whole of Asia before it could get there. A new Great Game was opening up that Russia seemed likely to win. British policy-makers observed with alarm the steady increase of commercial activity along the rivers Ob, Yenisei, Lena and Amur into northern China. By 1860 Russia had established settlements along the Sea of Okhotsk and the Sea of Japan, and Vladivostok was fast becoming a major centre - telegraph lines to Shanghai and Nagasaki were opened in 1871. The annexation of Korea became a target for both Russia and Japan – and from there the Russians felt they could gain access to the glittering prize of India. Naturally, the British viewed the Russians as a (perhaps exaggerated) dire threat to the heart of their empire; in due course, Alfred was presciently to recommend the annexation of two strategic bases....

When the Russian government makes its next move south, possession will doubtless be taken of Port Lazaref [107] in the Korean Territory, a port always free of ice, and to be able to coerce China on the one hand and Japan on the other. If Japan were troublesome Russia could seize Tsu Sima[108], a long-coveted possession[109]. To us Port Hamilton[110] and Tsu Sima would be invaluable, and no favourable opportunity should be lost of obtaining either one or the other.

Alfred's view was vindicated when, in 1885, the British occupied the islands of Komondo off the southern coast of Korean peninsula as a base to blockade the Russian fleet, and as an advanced station to support possible operations against Vladivostok.

However, before assuming his appointment, Alfred had some parochial duties to attend to. In June he hosted the Hambleden choir outing. The day was reported in the Parish Magazine....

The men of the choir went for their excursion on Wednesday June 3rd. Other trips and holidays of the choir have been successful and full of enjoyment, but none surpassed this. They drove in Mr Feesey's van to Maidenhead station[111], whence they had pleasure tickets to Paddington. At Paddington, our kind friend Admiral Ryder met us, and to his skilful and persevering guidance is due the most enjoyment we all received.

We first walked across the Park to the Albert Memorial, and admired the huge emblems of the four great Continents, the bas-reliefs with figures of all the great men of literature, science and art which the world has ever produced, as well as the elegant and beautiful design of the whole work.[112]

Thence we went to the Kensington Museum[113], where among so many other curiosities, we did not fail to pay our respects to

'King Coffee's Umbrella'[114]. We had not time for more than a passing admiration of the wonders of this museum.

The underground railway took us rapidly to Westminster[115]. To the Abbey of course we went. It was not a 'free' day for the chapels, but the Verger suggested that for a Choir no doubt the Canon in residence would give a 'free' order. The application of the Rector and the Admiral at the Canon's house had the desired effect; and without verger or any hindrance, we had leave to wander among and admire the extraordinary beauties of Henry VII's and other chapels.

Thence through Westminster Hall into two of the Courts adjacent, and then to the river. Here we went on board a steamer which took us rapidly past and through objects of the greatest interest – the Thames Embankment,[116] Somerset House, London Bridge, the Tower, with the shipping great and small, and landed us at Greenwich at 1.30. Dinner despatched, we visited the Painted Hall, shuddered at the naval engagements, paid our respects to Nelson's coat and sword, and then visited the models of ships etc.

By this time, it was 4.30. We took a steamer again, and returned to Hungerford Stairs, where Gatti's coffee house furnished us a sumptuous tea.[117]

Then our party broke up for a time. Some walked through Regent Street etc to Paddington[118]; some of us went with Admiral Ryder to visit the Newport Market Refuge for homeless and destitute boys which owes so much to his fostering care. Some went, but for a short time, to hear a concert in the Edgware Road. We met again (except for our good guide, who left us in Oxford Street to write half the night for the good of the public) at Paddington Station at 9 o'clock, at Maidenhead Station found the van ready for us, and at 12.30 found ourselves safe and sound in Hambleden again. The most enjoyable day we've ever had.

Such stamina!

So it was that in July 1874 Alfred arrived at Chatham to supervise the fitting out of his flagship *HMS Audacious* and to welcome her captain and his his second-in-command, Captain Philip Colomb, *possibly the most powerful and sensitive intellect of the nineteenth-century Navy*[119]. Alfred had personally selected Colomb to be his Number 2 as he (Colomb) had impressed as one of the most intellectual of all the flag officers. He had been one of the first to perceive that the vast changes which must ensue from the introduction of steam into the navy would necessitate a new system of signals and a new method of manoeuvres and tactics. He had written seminal works on both subjects, the last published only a few weeks before he set out for China with Alfred - the *Manual of Fleet Evolutions*. Alfred had been an advocate of such manoeuvres – he had referred to *steam evolutions* in his letter to his son, Eddy some six years previously, in 1868.

The *Manual* became a sacred text to many, but was criticised by some (notably Admiral Sir George Tyron, who, ironically, would be one of the 350 who perished when his flagship *HMS Victoria* collided with *HMS Camperdown* during manoeuvres in 1893) as marking the eclipse of Nelson's action-principles. Nevertheless, it opened the door to the complex and rapid fleetwork for which the main squadrons of the late Victorian Navy became famous. We are told that the *Manual...*

> *.... read like a glossary of ballet evolutions; elaborate, complex, spectacular and prohibitive of all initiative.*[120]

It was the anticipation of sharing ideas with Colomb that persuaded Alfred that he was the man who he wanted to spend the next three years of his life with on the *Audacious*.

The subsequent voyage to the East was a gentle affair, first stopping at Malta to pay his respects to Louie's grave, then through the recently opened Suez Canal, and thence via Galle and Penang to Singapore and Saigon, and finally Hong Kong in March 1875.

Despite numerous briefings before he took up his command, nothing could have prepared Alfred for Hong Kong. Ships were continually arriving and departing from all over the world: whalers that traversed the globe, cargo vessels in search of freight, East India merchantmen, Yankee tea clippers, opium despatch vessels, paddle steamers, P&O mail ships and, at any time, hundreds of Chinese junks and lorchas that ceaselessly plied between mainland China, Singapore and Hong Kong. And just as impressive as this crowded harbour were the wharves, bamboo jetties, warehouses and factories that massed on the water's edge. Alongside this orgy of trade and commerce grew the special businesses that served it – banks and law firms, insurance companies and shipbrokers, financiers and journalists, charlatans and whores.

The seedy atmosphere that permeated Hong Kong was exacerbated by the huge floating population that incessantly washed through its cramped streets and into its opium dens, gambling houses and brothels. Here in the narrow, jostling streets the visitor would take in the sights, sounds and smells of this young, frenetic city. Noses were assailed with the smells of food sizzling over open fires and incense emanating from joss houses and temples. Exotic fruit and vegetables filled market stalls; all sorts of birds, still alive were tied by their feet and suspended in the air; great mounds of fish lay on fishmongers' slabs. Live monkeys with their skulls cut open could be bought. Hambleden it was not!

Presiding over this mass of humanity were the British, headed by the Governor, Sir Arthur Kennedy. In the first hundred years as a Crown colony Hong Kong was an incredibly divided society. There were the obvious racial divisions between the British and the Chinese, which were not merely a matter of class and money, since some of the richest people on the island were Chinese. Despite their wealth, the rich Chinese businessmen did not socialise with their European counterparts of equal wealth and commercial attainments. On top of racial divisions, there were divisions among the British themselves, the most obvious was the split between the official class, with their elite culture, their classical education and their competence in the Chinese language, and the class of wealthy expatriate merchants, the taipans.

Somewhere between the senior officials and the merchants were of the 'cadet officers', or junior civil servants – a bureaucratic elite employed to replace the old Chinese Mandarins. But unlike the Mandarins who believed they had a paternal duty to treat the people under their administration like their own children, cadets only served a two-year period of duty, and often had barely a smattering of Cantonese. Unlike the senior civil servants, they did not come from aristocratic backgrounds – they came from a solid, though not rich, upper middle-class family, went to public school, but not to the most prestigious, and then went up to one of the older universities where they read classics or history and were noted for their application to study and their interest in healthy recreation. Thy acted like the prefects in the schools which had educated them. Ideas of protocol and precedence were of particular importance, as was proficiency in social skills – picnics, swimming parties, polo, golf, tennis and bridge.

The British established a reputation for pettiness, exclusivity, arrogance and high living. The taipans and cadets enjoyed the sort of extravagant lifestyle that could have only dreamed about had they lived in Britain. Social life centred around the Hong Kong Club, the touchstone of acceptability, from which *shop keepers, Chinese, Indians, women and other undesirables* were rigidly excluded. The Club sought to imitate the smartest clubs in London's Piccadilly or St James.

Such was the formality of social distinctions that a precedence table was established so that everyone knew his or her place, with the Governor at the top down to the Superintendent of the Botanical and Forestry Department at number 26. Alfred as a Rear Admiral commanding the China Station was only one below the Governor at number 2

Overlooking this melee was the craggy peak of Victoria, the home of prominent European residents who appreciated its panoramic view over the city and its temperate climate compared to the sub-tropical climate in the rest of Hong Kong. The Peak was not only a beautiful place; it also symbolised privilege and exclusivity. No Chinese except servants were allowed to live there, no matter how rich. For western observers it was a sort of English oasis in the midst of semi barbarism – a little piece of Surrey, complete with racecourse – apart from the sedan chairs and rickshaws that carried residents up and down the steep slopes. As Daniel

Defoe had observed some 150 years earlier, *He* (the Englishman) *does not accommodate himself to his surroundings; they have got to accommodate themselves to him.*

Alfred's immediate challenge was to diffuse an impending conflict between Japan, Russia and China over Korea which each saw as having the potential of another India. He met local officials in Saigon and Hong Kong, and then sailed to Woosung, part of modern Shanghai, arriving in February 1875 amid a huge rainstorm. Fortunately, rather like the weather, the crisis too proved to be a storm in a teacup.

Whereas Hong Kong was a British colony, regulated by British justice and administrators, Shanghai was a frontier town where local laws prevailed, apart from in the foreign enclave called the Bund. It was the Wild East! Like Hong Kong, it had a reputation for loucheness; a whiff of scandal always hung over both towns. Rumours abounded that the European elite never scrupled to do deals with local gangsters or get rich on shady government contracts. Like Melbourne or Bendigo, or a thousand American frontier towns, Shanghai boomed in a rather uncontrolled and haphazard way, apart from, of course, the Bund, the waterfront promenade with its palatial houses, clubs, consulates and commercial headquarters. Even then, it was one of the most famous addresses on the planet. But while some western inhabitants relaxed in their clubs playing endless games of billiards, in the narrow, muddy streets of the city could be found traders from all over the world, whose swell of humanity was parted by speeding, expressionless, sweating coolies toiling under prodigious weights or pulling a rickshaw. Meanwhile, offshore, moored British steel-hulled gunships, the officers of which became part of the social scene. As the South China Herald reported, at the annual regatta of the Shanghai Rowing Club…

> *By kind permission of Captain Colomb and the officers, the band of the Audacious played in the garden during the afternoon and contributed greatly to the pleasure of the visitors. The apposite introduction of a few bars of 'See the Conquering Hero Comes' while the winner of the Ladies Purse was being*

conducted to receive his prize, was not the least happy of their efforts[121].

Both cities stood for something important. The colonial grandeur of the settlements and the opulent ostentation of the expatriate merchants were intended to broadcast to the local population that the Western presence was permanent and highly lucrative...........and that China was powerless, and woe betide any 'native' that impeded western progress.

This was the mood when, some 1,200 miles away in Yunnan on the Burma-China border, an incident took place in November 1875 which resulted in the murder of a British consular official, one Augustus Margary. It appeared that Margary and four of his Chinese staff had been killed when surveying a possible railway line, and their heads hung on the town walls. It says something about the region's isolation that it took over six weeks for news of the 'Yunnan Outrage' to reach the British community in eastern China. Yet this was nothing compared to the eight months it took Britain to send an investigative mission to Yunnan. Much of the intervening time was wasted in angry posturing on the British diplomatic side, matched by skilful inaction by the Chinese authorities. Alfred's job was to maintain friendly relations with the Chinese while coping with such rantings as those written by the correspondent of Trewman's Exeter and Flying Post ....

All our talk today is of China, and of the chances that at the last moment Admiral Ryder with the Audacious will have to sail into the Yellow River, and to prove to Li Han Chang[122] that if there is no magic in diplomacy, there is a good deal of diplomacy in a rifled cannon. I do not believe the misunderstanding will end in war, and that is the opinion of Whitehall, but it may, for even the fate of the Summer Palace has not apparently taught the officials of the Yamen of Pekin that 'the foreign devils' are not men to be trifled with – that when they put their foot down and say they need this or that, they mean to have it, and that it is well to let them have it at once, especially if they begin to play with the hilt of their sword, and the great difficulty we have to face in dealing with the Court of Pekin is to know who is master, who rules the will of the Ruler, a woman, a eunuch or a minister.

It is quite possible that in ten minutes Mr Wade[123] might be able to tame the proud and haughty spirit of the white-buttoned Mandarin who recently kept him cooling his heels on the doorsteps of the Yamen till, out of temper, he got into his palanquin[124] again and returned home, and refused to call again till Li had apologised for the rudeness of his porter.

I hope that, however, if the worst comes to the worst, we shall this time act upon Prince Bismarck's rule, and make war pay for war. China is rich enough to pay, for what is the use of the Chancellor of the Exchequer plotting and contriving for surpluses, if, when the surplus is almost in his hands, it is to be frittered away on powder and shot?[125]

One of the cultural differences between the British and the Chinese relates to their different understanding of the concept of time. By 1855 the need to coordinate railway timetables meant that most towns in Britain had agreed to adopt a standard time (Greenwich Mean Time), though it was not until 1880 that a unified standard time for the whole of Great Britain achieved legal status. The measurement of time was important to the British; it became emblematic of the way in which the Victorians tried to regulate society. It was vital at sea. Although British mariners kept at least one chronometer on GMT to calculate their longitude from the Greenwich meridian, which was by convention considered to have longitude zero degrees, this did not affect shipboard time which was solar time. The Chinese, on the other hand, viewed the concept of time much more liberally; to this day China has only one time zone, although the United States, a country covering a similar number of degrees of longitude, has four. Consequently, the Chinese were used to having to wait; it was part of their culture, and leaving Mr Wade *cooling his heels on the doorstep* would not have seemed discourteous. Simply the way they did things there.

However, before Alfred could concentrate on resolving the Yunnan incident, his attention was diverted by another incident, this time in Perak. It was while at Shanghai that Alfred learned of the assassination of a British colonial official known as a 'Resident', a certain James Birch, in the Malay state of Perak. A Malay deputation had previously entreated with Governor-General Andrew Clarke in Singapore *to prevent the Resident from interfering with religion and custom, from acting without consulting the Sultan and chiefs, and from depriving them of their property, namely fugitive slaves and feudal dues.* Clarke observed that *I am very much annoyed with Birch and the heads-over-heels way in which he does things; he and I will come to sorrow yet, if he does not mind.* And sorrow it was, for on 2 November 1875 Birch was stabbed to death in his bathing house by one Dato' Maharajalela[126]. The *Audacious* was ordered from Hong Kong to Singapore *with two additional seven pounders and a large supply of Hale's rockets,* from where she transported the Naval Brigade to Perak. In February 1876 Alfred planned an attack on the insurgents' fortress, no doubt drawing on his own youthful adventures in Nicaragua. He later informed the Admiralty that ….

The heavy work of the seamen in the Perak consisted in poling the boats, laden with guns and ammunition, for many consecutive days, under a broiling tropical sun, where oars were of no use against a current running at the rate of four knots an hour, and in carrying guns, rockets and ammunition, in addition to their own accoutrements , through the jungle over roads so nearly impassable that only seven miles could be gained each day.

I have not received a single complaint of the conduct of the bluejackets and marines. For nearly a month the brigade had nothing to eat but preserved meat, supplemented occasionally by wild buffalo – no vegetables or bread. The men were constantly wet through with rain, and they had frequently to wade through water and mud over their waists. They followed the Malays through the jungle, from village to village, stockade

> *to stockade, never giving them time to occupy the latter in force.*[127]

By mid-1876, the war ended with the capture of prominent leaders and warriors, and Dato' Maharajalela was subsequently hanged. Two of his followers were exiled to the Seychelles; over two dozen sailors volunteered to escort them! Well, it beats wading through snake infested jungles.

Meanwhile, back in China, after weeks of negotiations by Wade and Alfred, a treaty was signed by Wade and Li on board *Audacious*, just off Cheefoo[128]. It gives some idea of the importance of China when we see the list of dignitaries who attended the signing ceremony: as well as Sir Thomas Wade, Alfred and several senior British and Chinese diplomats, there were Government Ministers from Russia, Germany, the United States, Spain, France, Austria & Hungary. During his visit to the flagship, Li was given a demonstration of its artillery, and was......

> *.... especially pleased with the use of electricity in firing off the guns, and asked permission to discharge a broadside by the electrical apparatus. He pressed his thumb firmly on the spring which brought out the spark, and as the united simultaneous sound of the great guns responded to his act, he could not withhold an exclamation of delight of having been a part instrument in the explosion.*[129]

One practical result of the treaty was that the Chinese official mission of apology to Britain became a permanent diplomatic mission, opening the way for a permanent foreign representation of China, the first in modern times to any western nation. The Chinese felt they could submit their apology without any loss of face as a few months earlier, Disraeli added the title of Empress of India to Queen Victoria, a title that provided further proof of Disraeli's claim that Britain was an 'Asiatic' power, since Japan, Russia and the Ottoman realms were all ruled by emperors and China was ruled by Empress Cixi. It demonstrated that Britain was serious and determined to maintain its position on the continent of Asia. The Chinese apology was therefore given to a greater being – someone superior to a mere queen, Victoria *Regina et Imperatrix*.

A midshipman on *Audacious* remembered the impression that Li created when he came on board the flagship with 200 officials:

> *his dignified height, his majestic bearing, his piercing eyes that seemed to see everything at once, all combining to make an unforgettable impression.*

While in Shanghai, Alfred managed to get himself embroiled in a controversy concerning the establishment of a Lock Hospital. Lock Hospitals had been established in England under the Contagious Diseases Acts of 1864-69 in an attempt to preserve the health of soldiers and sailors by permitting policemen in ports and army towns to detain any woman (though in reality, mostly prostitutes) suspected of venereal infection. She would then be compelled to have checks for venereal disease, and if found to be infected, was placed in a locked hospital until 'cured'. Alfred, naturally, concerned about the welfare of his men, advised the local Municipal Council of what he considered to be the positive results of Lock Hospitals in England, Singapore and Hong Kong. Consequently, a Lock Hospital was opened in Shanghai on 1 January 1877 - but not without controversy. Not, though, the controversy that one may imagine - that the concept was grossly unfair to women in order to protect the health of men. If the priority had been to fight venereal disease, then inspecting the prostitutes' clients should also have been required by the Acts. However, the assumption was that, while men would be offended at the intrusion, the women were already so degraded that further humiliations were of no consequence.

No, the controversy that Alfred faced in Shanghai was that even a discussion about a Lock Hospital gave offence to many of the settlement's inhabitants who cringed when the seamier side of the community's activities were bared, with the subsequent implication that Shanghai was a port 'dangerous to sailors.' Moreover, Alfred's attitude was resented. Although it was agreed he was well intended, it was later commented that

> *There was something ludicrous in Admiral Ryder's patronage of the Council, and the effusiveness with which he patted it on the back. Yet much may be forgiven for an amiable but rather fussy old gentleman who acted in all honesty.*[130]

Reynolds may also have added that while the Admiral had sailed away permanently, the settlement's expenses incurred by the Lock Hospital sailed on. Nevertheless, the Hospital continued until 1910.

The movements of the China fleet were widely reported in the British press; the country took pride in the flag-waving exploits of its admirals in far flung parts of the world. It also learned, however, that in May 1877 there were reports of Alfred being *very unwell, and will probably be compelled to resign his command.* He sailed to Yokohama where *he will remain for a few weeks.* Later he would write that he was suffering from angina pectoris, and was in agony for days on end. In fact, his period of command would continue for another six months, during which time he was promoted to a full admiral. He left Hong Kong on 8 November 1877, and arrived home in January the following year......

.... but, sadly, too late to be at the funeral of his son, Eddy. During Eddy's early years, Alfred had written several beautifully illustrated letters to him, but these had effectively ended in 1862[131]when the boy was nine. Despite the affection shown in his letters – he referred to himself as 'Papa' or 'your affectionate father', and to Eddy as 'my own dear little boy', 'my darling boy' and 'dearest Eddy' - Alfred's relationship with his son as he grew older had not been easy. After the death of his wife when his son was just two and a half, his career meant that Alfred spent long periods away from home, during which time Eddy was raised and educated by relatives and governesses at Hambleden and Launde Abbey. Unsurprisingly, perhaps, he tended to exhibit certain dysfunctional personality traits, not least those relating to his social and emotional development. Being used to being solitary, he was antisocial and awkward in company, especially male company, and had a difficult time of it when he was sent to Eton. There he had to learn the hard way of the compromises and the rules that are generally the hallmarks of a public-school education, not to mention the bullying and other character-forming rituals. It must have been a horrible experience for a boy brought up predominantly by women. Consequently, it is likely that he grew up to be a disturbed young man, who had to live in the shadow of an increasingly distinguished, and absent, father - in his death certificate, Eddy's 'rank or profession' was listed simply as *Son of Admiral Alfred Phillips Ryder RN*. There was talk of him going up to Oriel College, Oxford, the alma mater of Sir George Grey, but this came to nothing. Instead he became a law student at his uncles' law practice.

The Hambleden Parish Magazine records him playing cricket for the village against the estate and domestic workers of Greenlands, WHS's country home, in August 1874. This was possibly the last time he and his father were together, for Alfred departed for China in October. The Hambleden Rector thoroughly approved of the game....

> *The young men cannot do better than spend their leisure time of an evening in the cricket field. The game of cricket is a thoroughly manly and sensible amusement.*[132]

One may imagine that Alfred shared these sentiments, as do we all!

Eddy had married Agnes Bickley in June 1877 at the fashionable St Andrew's Church, Wells Street, Marylebone, a marriage of which Alfred let it be known from China that he did not approve. It says something about Eddy's relationship with his father that despite understanding that Alfred did not favour the marriage, and knowing that he would be back from China within months, Eddy still went ahead and married Agnes. We may surmise that Agnes, knowing that the marriage may well not take place once Alfred returned, put pressure on Eddy to marry soon. And Eddy, used to acceding to older women, complied. It was a measure of how much the father – son relationship had broken down.

Alfred must have felt personally affronted and let down. The role of a Victorian patriarch was to be obeyed. He had reckoned Eddy to be too young for marriage at just twenty-four, especially as Agnes was thirty-three, and judged that she was not of his social standing. Her father was described in the 1861 census as a 'landed proprietor'. In any case, the marriage was not to last long, for Eddy died only three months later at his home at 5, Victoria Street, London. His death certificate described the cause of death as *pleurisy and effusion (7days), probably thrombosis (2 hours),* which is essentially fluid in the lungs, followed by a fatal blood clot. The commonest cause of this in 1877 would have been TB for which there was no effective treatment until the early 1950s. Agnes never married again. After Eddy died, she lived with her widowed mother in Warwick Road, Paddington, and was living in Plymouth when she died on 5th July 1924 aged 79. Eddy had left her an income of £300 pa out his estate.

Incidentally, TB is on the increase again in the UK - immigration, HIV and homelessness being deemed to be the culprits.

Alfred was stunned - both his wife and son lost to the same illness. We can only imagine his anguish. He arranged for a memorial to Eddy to be placed in the chapel at Launde Abbey, and for him to be buried in Hambleden adjacent to the grave of his grandmother. The graves are in direct line of sight from the family house, past which members of his family would walk on their way to church. It was Alfred's way of keeping his son part of the family, and assuaging the guilt he felt for all the years that he had been too distant from him.

8

Portsmouth

*So he fed them according to the integrity of his heart; and
guided them by the skilfulness of his hands.*
Psalm 78:72

When Alfred arrived back in England, he found a few things had
changed. Firstly, he found Britain, indeed Europe, was gripped in
an agricultural depression.

It was rooted in transport improvements which allowed the shipping
of wool and frozen meat from Australasia, and, above all, of bulk
grain from the American plains to glut European markets. Seemingly
unlimited grain imports meant that farmers could no longer rely upon
high prices when harvests failed, and a succession of harvest failures in
the late 1870s underlined their vulnerability. Railways had opened up the
American prairies, the Russian plains and the Australian outback; cheap
long-distance steamship transport allowed the invasion of European
markets which had previously been protected by high transport costs.

In two decades from 1875 cereal prices halved; some parts of the
country suffered widespread rural depopulation as local traders and
craftsmen graduated to the towns. Hambleden did not escape. Its
agriculture had been based for centuries on the so called 'triple division of
land tenure'. A landowner owned the land, which was worked by tenant
farmers who paid a rental income to the landowners, and who in turn
employed agricultural labourers. There was an understanding, often
friendship and affection, between those at the top and those at the bottom
of this hierarchy. All would happily sing

The rich man in his castle,
The poor man at his gate,

He made them, high or lowly,
And ordered their estate.

All things bright and beautiful,
All creatures great and small,
All things wise and wonderful:
The Lord God made them all.

This type of landownership made efficiencies of scale and investment in the land, in new equipment and methods of production, possible. Everyone had a vested interest in increasing the profitability of the land – and everyone suffered in the bad times.

So it was in Hambleden. The economy of the village was based on a seasonal cycle of production, comprising long months of cultivation followed by short periods of harvest. The length of the cycle of production and the timing of the harvest were determined by the weather – the fundamental uncertainty of agriculture. Each morning workers would sniff the air, check the direction of the wind and strain their eyes into the sky to try to determine whether the harvest would be sufficient this year to feed their families. That Britain was able to feed its growing urban industrial population was down to the villagers of Hambleden, and thousands like them, ploughing fields, clearing ground, digging irrigation ditches, sowing crops, carrying water buckets and sweating.

In 1877 the centre of the village was dominated by Hambleden Farm[133], tenanted by Fred Biggs with his wife, Hannah, and three young children, the only farm in the village. The remains of some of the outbuildings can still be seen to the rear. The movement of cattle through the village was a daily occurrence as they were gathered in for milking. Sheep would also pass through as they were moved from one grazing ground to another. And, of course, horses were as common as motor vehicles are today. Although the village contains no farms today, farm clusters, both ancient and modern, are dotted around the countryside nearby - at Mill End, Rotten Row, Pheasants' Hill, Burrow, Rockwell End, Bacres, Huttons and Colstrope. Some are still working farms and are virtually unchanged since the nineteenth century; other, smaller, farms have been absorbed into larger ones and some have become private dwellings. In 1877, all these farms were on the estate of one or other of the two principal landowners - WH Smith, who had acquired the Greenlands estate in 1868, and Charles Scott-Murray, the owner of the Manor House and the Hambleden Estate. Most villagers lived in a house owned by one or other of these estates or worked on a tenanted farm, and so were particularly vulnerable to downturns in the agricultural economy.

The Rector attempted to explain the economics to his parish….

> The present agricultural distress which prevails so widely in this country is not really caused by bad harvests, but by keen competition from abroad, and consequently by the low price of all kinds of corn. There is plenty in the land, and the poor can have a cheap loaf, but those who grow the corn cannot possibly make an adequate profit out of it. Perhaps if corn were dearer, wages would be higher, and more labour would be employed, so that after all a very cheap loaf may not be the greatly earthly blessing.[134]

I'm sure they went away happy!

Fortunately, such was the magnanimity of the two landowners that suffering was kept to a minimum. But suffering there was. Alfred could see it when he returned to Hambleden. When he was elsewhere, he could read about it in the Parish Magazine…….

> A long and trying corn harvest because of the stormy weather. A good crop, though prices are low.[135]

> After very unsettled weather at harvest time, it would be well if we were to meet together **in larger numbers** and humbly with one heart and voice, were to ask Almighty God to help us in our distress.[136] (original emphasis)

> Heavy rain has delayed the harvest.[137]

> Harvest Festival on Nov 7. Some members of the congregation were late as the church clock, by whose time the service was held, was fast.[138]

> *It has been very wet – we are in **His** hands.[139] (original emphasis)*

Rain was not always a bad thing, though. In August 1878, Alfred would read

> *The excessive heat of late has wonderfully ripened the crops, but the thunder rain that has just fallen is a great blessing to many of our parishioners on the hills, who were beginning to get short of water. The people at Rockwell End and Pheasants Hill are very grateful for the kind assistance that has been afforded them.*

The other thing that had changed was that his Hambleden neighbour, William Henry Smith (WHS) had become First Lord of the Admiralty in Disraeli's cabinet. WHS had joined the family news agency business (instead of taking holy orders) at the age of sixteen, and had assumed control of it on the death of his father in 1865. The repeal of the newspaper stamp duty in 1854 had given an enormous impetus to the circulation of journals, and W. H. Smith & Son were in a position to derive immediate advantage from it. WHS had secured, at what was considered by his father an extravagant outlay, a lease of the blank walls in all the principal railway stations for advertising – revolutionary at the time. This led to negotiations with the different railway companies for the right to erect bookstalls at their stations, and by 1862 he had secured the exclusive rights of selling books and newspapers on all the important stations in England. Profits steadily grew till they became prodigious[140] – and all without resorting to selling the pernicious literature which had hitherto made railway bookstalls notorious.

The Morning Post congratulated Disraeli for showing *the discrimination which has invariably enabled him to put the right man in the right place* when he appointed WHS as First Lord, and the Hambleden Parish Magazine offered him congratulations and *rejoiced that the country has the benefit of his sound wisdom.* Nevertheless, the appointment was greeted with some sharp criticism from his own party; he was a mere tradesman while previous holders of the position had been persons of high rank. The incongruity of the choice found popular expression in the comic opera of *H.M.S. Pinafore*, and WHS spent the rest of his career with the nickname of Pinafore Smith. However, his appointment belied all misgivings and proved a complete success; it was said of him that although he was slow in forming a judgment, he had the enviable gift, once it was formed, of adhering to it without anxiety. Few men have secured so much honest respect from the House of Commons, owed not to brilliant qualities of debate, but to sterling sound sense and perfect integrity. 'Punch' in its weekly sketches of parliament, conferred on him the sobriquet of 'Old Morality.'

WHS had bought the Greenlands estate, which included a substantial riverside mansion, in 1868. He made considerable additions to the house, both internally and externally, creating a lovely walled garden and various outbuildings – stables, garages, workshops. Greenlands had 26 servants, and accommodation for them and estate workers was built in Dairy Lane. His improvements to the house received a cool reception from Jerome K. Jerome who joked in Three Men in a Boat that it was *the rather uninteresting-looking river residence of my newsagent.* Be that as it may, WHS became Hambleden's greatest benefactor; apart from improvements and additions to the village infrastructure (a new school, the schoolmaster's house, an institute for the young men) he contributed to local charities: a clothing club, blankets for the poor, a savings club,

Such was his attachment to the village that he insisted that the weddings of his daughters and stepdaughters should take place in the parish church rather than a more fashionable London venue. And the villagers loved it! In February 1879, his stepdaughter, Mary Auber Leach, married Captain William Codrington RN, private secretary to First Lord of the Admiralty, one William Henry Smith – a case of marrying the boss's daughter! Later he would be promoted to be Captain of the Steam Reserve at Portsmouth and then Captain of the Gunnery School – in which positions he would report to Alfred as C in C Portsmouth. Later he would be promoted to Rear Admiral. Sadly, William and Mary were only to be married for nine years for William died in July 1888 and became the last person to be buried in Hambleden Churchyard. He had been forty-seven when they got married; she was twenty-two. His comrades presented a magnificent lectern to the church in his memory – still in use today. Mary outlived him by forty-two years, dying in 1930.

We think that we may safely say that never, certainly within the memory of any living person, has our quiet little village been in so quiet a state as on the 2nd January, on the occasion of the marriage of Miss Leach, step daughter of the Right Hon W H Smith of Greenlands with Capt. Codrington RN. The day was perfect for the season of the year.

It had been preceded by a wet and stormy night. Great preparations had been made, among which was the erection of an awning from the lychgate on the churchyard path to the church door. This had been put up the evening before amidst heavy rain. Just at midnight, under the combined influences of a high wind and a great weight of snow, the whole thing fell, with much damage to the framework, and the canvas became so hard with the frost that it was absolutely useless.

As the day turned out, the sky afforded a much better covering than any awning.

Just after 11 o'clock the bridal party began to arrive. The service was performed at the chancel-step by the Rector, who was assisted by the Rev Sir Emelius Bayley, Vicar of St Johns, Paddington, of which parish Mr Smith is a churchwarden.

After the blessing, the clergy, the bride and bridegroom, followed by the eight bridesmaids, and attended by Mr and Mrs Smith, proceeded to the Communion rails while the choir and congregation chanted the psalm.

When the service was concluded and the registers were signed, the bridal party returned in proper procession, and were greeted with rice strewn in their path in place of flowers.

The wedding breakfast was, as might be expected, elegant and well served. The presents were numerous and handsome. Those which evidently gave the keenest pleasure to the receivers were those presented by the servants of the family, and by the out-of-door workmen (gardeners, labourers, woodmen etc); of these the bridegroom made special mention in returning thanks for drinking his and Mrs Codrington's health. A little after 3 pm the happy pair drove off amid a shower of old shoes and rice.

There were about 30 carriages and 50 horses in Hambleden at one time.

About 4 pm the children of the parish had begun to assemble in force (at Greenlands). Shortly after, they were admitted to the sight of two gorgeous Christmas trees, such as most of them had never seen before, blazing with many lights, and glittering with presents, oranges, crackers and sugar plums. There was a present for every child and every teacher. In about an hour all was over, the candles burning low. Each child took a bun away, and all parents, who had had special invitations, and the children were greatly delighted.

The bells had kept the ears merry throughout the day. Captain Codrington heard the early peel at Greenlands as he was getting up.

The day following there was a great feasting for the labourers on the estate, followed by a dance which was kept up to a late hour.[141]

WHS' funeral in 1891 was the largest event the village had ever known. (It still is!) He had died at Walmer Castle near Deal in Kent, his home as Lord Warden of the Cinque Ports, and his body was transported from there by rail, finally arriving at Henley......

At Henley Station the coffin was placed in a hearse with stained glass panels, and amid demonstrations of respect conveyed to Hambleden, where the interment subsequently took place. As the cortege proceeded along the route, about 100 carriages representing the principal gentry in the neighbourhood joined the procession, which was nearly half a mile in extent, and blinds were drawn at private residences, and in Henley business was partly suspended, the bells of the two local churches tolling in the meantime. Arrived at the lichgate of St Mary's Churchyard, Hambleden, some four miles distant, the corpse was met by the officiating clergy, the Rev. North Pinder (Rural Dean) and the Rev. C M Wetherell (rector of the parish), and the surpliced choir from St Paul's Church, Knightsbridge, who led the way into the sacred edifice, where the first portion of the solemn service was gone through. Afterwards a rather long journey had to be accomplished to the cemetery[142], which presented a dismal aspect after heavy rain. The service was concluded, the coffin being lowered during a heavy shower; and tears were shed by many of the large number of onlookers present during the singing of the hymn 'Now the labourer's task is o'er'.[143]

Second only to the Smiths in their benevolence to the village was the Ryder family. Barely a month went by without the Parish Magazine recording some donation to a local cause – the clothing society, the school, building of new chapels in nearby Frieth and Lane End and so on. No sooner had Alfred arrived back from China than he was donating three guineas to a fund to purchase a false arm for the one James Harvey lost in an accident. A total of £34 was collected.

In 1879 a scheme to renovate the church tower was relaunched by Alfred and WHS. The scheme had started back in 1873, when

Through the kindness of Admiral Ryder, photographs have been taken of the church tower as it is now, and as at the restoration of the church it was proposed to be altered by the architect H Woodyer[144]. The photographs have been hung in the vestry for all to inspect.[145]

Alfred was then posted to China, so the scheme was put on the back-burner until 1879....

> We need to improve the appearance of Hambleden Church Tower, which is later than the church itself, and has no architectural merit. Admiral Ryder and Mr Smith had had some plans prepared, but then the Admiral was called to China, and all plans were suspended. Now the subject has come forward again and Mr Smith has donated £500 and the Admiral £100.

The fund received a boost when Alfred's friend, the long serving Rector Ridley died, and it was decided to dedicate the renovated tower to his memory[146]. Such was the esteem in which he was held that many villagers donated small amounts, some as little as tuppence; many of sixpence - truly the widow's mite. Alfred, who had assumed the role of treasurer, donated another £100. Other members of the family donated a further £35. By May 1883 work was well under way, when it was decided that they might as well restore the bells while the tower was encased in scaffolding – another £80! More contributions were made, and the restored tower and bells were inaugurated later that year. We can see and hear the results of their efforts to this day.

We have seen how Alfred and WHS had worked together for the good of Hambleden. It is not too fanciful to think that there would have been a certain amount of social interaction between the two families as they only lived a couple of miles apart (a twenty-minute walk through the woods and across the fields as the crow flies). However, the first mention of the two of them together in a professional capacity was in May 1878 when Alfred attended three receptions and dinners at the Admiralty, hosted by WHS. Later, in August, Alfred accompanied WHS when he presented prizes at the Royal Naval School at New Cross[147]. Later WHS would write to Alfred concerned about the reduced numbers of cadets in the Navy.

We have noted Alfred's concern for fallen women – the Newport Street Refuge and the Lock Hospital in Shanghai - and now he had the time to extend his patronage. His donations (£100) had been instrumental in establishing St Thomas' Home for the Friendless and Fallen in Basingstoke, which provided accommodation for up to 48 young women, aged between the ages of fifteen and thirty. Its aim was to provide a convent-based home for penitent 'fallen' women, and to provide them with *the chance of recovering the character they have lost before God and society*. The institution was run by Anglican nuns on behalf of the Church Penitentiary Society. The women were trained in needlework, laundry, cooking and dairy work. Now, following their successful partnership in restoring the church tower in Hambleden, he instructed Henry Woodyer again to design a new chapel in Basingstoke, which was opened in 1885[148].

Other interests of Alfred at this time included joining the executive committee of the Church Defence Institution, an earnest *association of Clergy and Laity for defensive and general purposes*. It strived towards greater unity within the Church of England and a desire to protect it from decline – topics that continue to resonate strongly within the Church today. It held lectures, produced literature and generally promoted and protected the role of the Church in society.

However, it was clear that, at only fifty-eight years old, Alfred still wished to be employed. He set wheels in motion, and in September 1878 received the following reply from WHS, First Lord…

> *My Dear Admiral*
>
> *I shall not fail to bear in mind as long as I continue in the Admiralty that you are still willing to serve and it will give me very great pleasure if it is within my power with due regard to the claims of other officers, to offer you employment.*[149]

Perhaps it came as little surprise then when, in November 1879, he was honoured to be appointed to the prestigious position of Commander in Chief, Portsmouth, with command of the south coast from Newhaven in East Sussex to Portland in Dorset.

The status of the Command meant he often had to entertain very distinguished visitors, for which he was given the use of the elegant Admiralty House, one of the first houses in the country to be fitted with a flush toilet. To be the senior officer of the largest port of the world's largest navy - the largest naval port in the world - was both a ceremonial and a functional position.

Functionally, he oversaw the completion of the complex rebuilding of the docks. The changeover to metal hulls not only required new building techniques, but also heralded a dramatic and ongoing increase in the potential size of new vessels, and the dockyards found themselves having to expand. In 1867 work had begun on three new interconnected basins, each of 14–22 acres. Each basin served a different purpose: ships would proceed from the repairing basin, to the rigging basin, to the fitting-out basin, and exit from there into a new tidal basin, ready to take on fuel alongside the sizeable coaling wharf there. Three dry docks were also constructed as part of the plan, as well as a parallel pair of sizeable locks for entry into the basin complex. A pumping station was built which not only served to drain these docks and locks, but also to deliver compressed air to power cranes, caissons and capstans.

We should not underestimate the complexity of the dockyards that came within Alfred's jurisdiction. Steel-hulled, steam-driven warships were at the cutting edge of Victorian technology, and the yards in which they were built also needed to be state of the art. A modern equivalent would be the yard in Rosyth on the Forth where the aircraft carrier HMS Queen Elizabeth was built.

Works were completed by 1881, and in July of that year Alfred was able to welcome Queen Victoria's grandsons, Princes William II and Henry of Prussia to Portsmouth to inspect *HMS Inflexible*, then the last word in naval construction and commanded by Captain (Jackie) Fisher[150].

Like Fisher himself, *Inflexible* seemed poised between the old and the new. She had masts and rigging, so looked familiar enough – in fact the sails were never used for propulsion, but because a ship's performance was partly judged on the speed with which a ship could set sails, Fisher was obliged to drill the crew in their use. But in other respects, she was hyper-modern. She mounted the largest guns and had the thickest armour ever to be fitted to a Royal Navy ship; no gun then in existence could pierce it. She was also the first Royal Navy ship to be completely lit by electricity[151], and the first to have underwater torpedo tubes. Controversially though, her bow and stern were unarmoured; she was designed so that if her un-armoured ends should be seriously damaged in action and become water-logged, the buoyancy of the armoured centre section of the ship would keep her afloat and upright. She was only to see action once, taking part in the bombardment of Alexandria in 1882 during which the blast from her own guns did considerable damage to her own infrastructure and boats. As Wellington had said in another context *'I don't know what effect they have upon the enemy, but, by God, they frighten me'!*

Later that year Alfred accompanied Princess Victoria, the eldest daughter of Queen Victoria (and mother of the two princes who had visited the dockyard in July) when she launched *HMS Canada*, the first all steel ship to be built in the yard.

His position meant he was in the forefront of innovative ideas – in June 1880 he oversaw a new system of deep-sea diving, designed by the pioneering diving engineer Henry Fleuss. Although his novel idea subsequently became a success, on this occasion the tender capsized and all the equipment was lost. As was reported…

> *The two sailors, wonderful to relate, could swim(!), but the apparatus, fulfilling its destiny, went to the bottom.*
>
> (My exclamation mark.)

In the same month, Alfred oversaw *'a series of very interesting torpedo experiments'* in Portchester Creek, during which he and his distinguished guests were accompanied on the viewing launch by a number of ladies! We can only imagine that the testing of torpedoes, causing as they did *'magnificent columns of water suddenly to rise some 200 or 300 feet in the air, the effect being particularly striking'*[152] was some sort of social event.

Apart from meeting and greeting various dignitaries as they crossed to and from the Isle of Wight to attend the Queen at Osborne, hosting foreign admirals and heads of state as they received guided tours of the fleet (including, as we have seen, the future Emperor of Germany, William II, with whom Britain would have some differences in 1914), and himself attending dinner with the Queen at Osborne on at least two occasions, Alfred's ceremonial duties included hosting a number of fashionable balls and dinners at Admiralty House, all of which were covered in detail in the press, rather in the same way as gossip magazines report on the activities of celebrities(!) today. In most instances, the horticulture seemed as important as the ladies' gowns.

In April 1880…

> *Some of the dresses were very handsome. One of white satin and striped gauze was gracefully draped with loops of mauve satin and sprays of white and coloured lilac. A black lace and satin dress had bows of red satin and clusters of white lilacs, and was worn with a large red bow in the hair, and a spray of white lilac. A blue silk dress had the sleeves composed of a large bow of blue satin ribbon. Most of the young ladies wore white dresses.[153]*

Another ball was held in the following month, at which about 250 guests attended…

> *The ballroom was decorated with choice hothouse plants. Dancing commenced at Half-past nine o'clock, and was kept up until about half-past two o'clock.[154]*

In February 1881….

> *The decorations and indeed the whole of the arrangements were most complete, the plants and flowers which were placed in every available space near the reception corridor especially giving a cool and refreshing aspect to the scene.*

> *The fine ballroom had been prepared for the occasion, special attention being paid to the polishing of the floor, and when dancing was at its height the scene was brilliant and gay in the extreme. There was a fine collection of camelias and azaleas on the large mantel above the chief stove, and on the sideboard was a splendid arrangement of pot plants, over which there was another pile of foliage plants immediately in front of the*

> *orchestral band. Supper was laid in the dining room, which was tastefully embellished.*[155]

Later that year, in December four hundred guests comprising General His Serene Highness Prince Edward of Saxe-Weimar, the commander in chief of the military garrison at the port, all principal naval and military officers of the port, and a large number of the great and good of Portsmouth began to arrive at nine thirty, and by ten o'clock the ballroom was......

> *...well filled. Dancing was kept up with unflagging spirit until two o'clock in the morning. The ballroom was profusely decorated with the choicest flowering and foliage plants, which were most artistically arranged, and presented a very beautiful appearance. The room was handsomely fitted up with the flags of all nations, trophies of arms, shields etc. A recherché supper was served at half past eleven in the dining room, the tables being prettily set out with all kinds of delicacies and ornamented with flowers in full bloom* (note, this was December!)

One of Alfred's final dinners at Portsmouth was a farewell dinner to retiring Vice-Admiral Fitzgerald A.C. Foley in April 1882. It was the one that gave him the most pleasure as the guests included his elderly sister Anna[156] and her husband Sir George Grey[157], his brother Spencer's widow, Julia, and her two daughters Una and Mary, the Codrington's, whose wedding he had attended three years earlier in Hambleden, and his good friend and number two from China, Captain Philip Colomb. The conversation must have included Hambleden gossip – the Greys, Ryders and Codrington's were very familiar with the place and Una had been born there. The others must have wondered what was this place that seemed to have such a hold over Alfred's family. It is rather how outsiders see villagers today.

But none of the distinguished visitors could have had quite the enjoyment and drama of the Hambleden choir on their outing in June 1880.......

Nothing could surpass their enjoyment of all they saw. They had, on their way to Reading, an adventure which might have been serious. At Caversham, in a narrow piece of road, the van was run against by a cart and the springs injured, so that the travellers had to proceed to Reading on foot or as they best could.

They were furnished with Pleasure Tickets from the Great Western and South-Western Railway Companies, and reached Portsmouth in the middle of the day. At the station they were met by messengers from Admiral Ryder, who conducted them to the Admiralty House where a handsome dinner was provided for them.

They were then divided into two groups, marked with red and blue ribbons respectively. They saw all the winders of the dockyard, including four of the finest ships in the world. They had to work hard, tramping it incessantly till past 6 pm, when after a cup of coffee, they re-entered their carriages at the station, reaching Reading again shortly after 9pm where they had supper.

All would have been perfect but for the foolish and wilful misconduct of two boys, who got separated from the rest, starting off homeward by themselves. As far as Caversham they got on all right, but there they took a wrong road and went to Emmer Green instead of Play Hatch. Meanwhile all the others, ignorant of what these two had done, were scouring Reading in search of them, and did not leave Reading till after midnight, having given full instructions to the Police.

These silly boys little foresaw the consequences of their wilfulness. They themselves wandered the whole night, while the others did not reach Hambleden till 2 am, and the poor parents were left till 8 am later that morning wondering what had become of their children. They got home just as some of the elders had started out afresh in quest of them.

> *The other members of the choir have determined, we think quite rightly, that they will not again go for an excursion in the company of these two boys, for they had been troublesome, more or less, during the whole day.*

Life was not all fun and festivities. In 1880 Alfred was asked to chair a Committee of Enquiry into the loss of *HMS Atalanta*, to enquire whether the ship was 'sound, stable and seaworthy', and to provide for the relatives of the crew.

Atalanta was serving as a training ship when in 1880 she disappeared with her entire crew of 280 souls after setting sail from Bermuda for Falmouth on 31 January. It was presumed that she sank in a powerful storm which crossed her route a couple of weeks after she sailed. The search for evidence of her fate attracted worldwide attention, and the Admiralty received more than 150 telegrams and 200 personal calls from anxious friends and relatives after it was announced that the ship was missing, and possibly lost. The most devastating verdict on the disaster was delivered by The Times...

> *...the criminal folly of sending some 300 lads who have never been to sea before in a training ship without a sufficient number of trained or experienced seamen to take charge of her in exceptional circumstances. The ship's company of the Atalanta numbered only about 11 able seamen, and when we consider that young lads are often afraid to go aloft in a gale to take down sail... a special danger attaching to the Atalanta becomes apparent.* [158]

Unlike other shipping disasters, neither survivors nor debris were ever found. Some modern analysts have identified the tragedy as a victim of the Bermuda Triangle phenomenon. However, Alfred's committee found that the *Atalanta* was a very stable ship and spoke favourably of her officers and crew; they pointed out that at the time of her loss exceptional storms proved fatal to a number of merchant vessels. Over £9,000 was raised for the bereaved families.

Because of his experience in charge of the Coast Guard in the 1860s, Alfred was the perfect person to be asked by the Society of Arts to chair an investigation into collisions of seamers in fog. He reported in May 1884 that such accidents were caused by steamers cutting corners (literally) and ignoring nautical regulations. They were driven by competition and the demand from passengers, shippers of freight and the general public for the quick delivery of mails. Simply, he said, captains of steamers must obey existing regulations that were perfectly adequate. He had had good cause to rely on these regulations during his career....

Sailing in a fog is like walking in a dark room, or in a light room with your eyes blindfolded. You have to be very cautious not to run against furniture which with us are rocks, banks of sand, the land, or against other people who have their eyes also blindfolded which with us are other ships. We make all kinds of strange noises to prevent other ships from running against us. We beat drums and blow horns to show we are going in one direction, and keep on ringing a bell if we are going in the other.[159]

Later he elaborated....

I told you in my last letter how dangerous a thick fog is at sea. The only wonder is that more accidents don't happen. Fogs are much thicker on water than on land. And if two ships run against one another in a fog, the weakest is very likely to go down to the bottom. We make all kinds of precautions (see above). If we are steaming, we have a steam whistle like the Engines in the Railway and we make it squeak fearfully.[160]

So, he was a bit of an expert.

Fittingly, a farewell ball was held at Admiralty House in October 1882 for Alfred's retirement; he formally retired on 27 November, at just sixty-two. In May 1884 as part of the Queen's birthday honours, he was, belatedly, appointed as a Knight Commander of the Most Honourable Order of the Bath as a 'fitting recognition'[161] of his services. His shoulder was tapped by the Queen at Windsor on July 11. One further honour awaited him – that of promotion to the honorary rank of Admiral of the Fleet in April 1885.

9

At the End of the Day

Who can find a virtuous woman? For her price is far above
rubies.

Proverbs 31:10

As with many people, men especially, retirement did not come easily
for Alfred. His work had brought him a sense of usefulness, a
sense of having contributed to the greater good of the nation. His sense
of self-worth was tied up very strongly in his naval career, and with
retirement he struggled to understand who he was and what was his
value. It was as though he had fallen off a cliff; his opinions were no longer
sought and his abilities were no longer recognised. No longer did he have
the structure of the Navy, the camaraderie of his crew and colleagues, his
social network. And being a senior officer and a high achiever, one used
to mixing with the great and the good, who had dined with the Queen, he
missed the attention, the admiration and the respect that had contributed
to his feelings of identity. Alastair Campbell, the former Prime Minister's
Director of Communications has said after he left Downing Street 'I
didn't know what to do with my life. At the time. I was quite profoundly
suicidal. It was all a bit weird'.[162]

Any major change in life, such as retirement, can cause stress; stress
is a primary cause of depression, a depression in Alfred's case not helped
by his anxiety over his suspected angina and the constant pain in his
back from his years at sea. So it is perhaps not surprising that his loss
of bearings and change of lifestyle contributed to a prolonged period of
depression. It was to seek advice for this complaint from a Dr Ogle of
Cavendish Square that Alfred was in London on that fateful day in April
1888. He had complained of sleeplessness, loss of memory, giddiness and

bumping into furniture. Significantly, he complained to Dr Ogle of 'a fear of some brain disease'. His father had died of chronic fatigue and lack of energy caused by the stress of overwork, and Alfred was afraid that he might have a similar disease. Today we might recognise his symptoms as early stage dementia.

Even today dementia is little understood. We know it covers a broad category of brain diseases that cause a long-term and often gradual decrease in the ability to think and remember. Such a decline is great enough to affect a person's daily functioning, more than one would expect due to aging. Until 1907 when the German psychiatrist Alois Alzheimer was able to identify a series of plaques and tangles in the brain, it was regarded as a form of madness, and sufferers were confined to asylums or hospitals.

The Victorians were preoccupied with madness. The country regarded itself as at the forefront of western civilisation, predicated on the notion of rationalism – or the absence of madness. To be mad was to be a 'non-being'; in the golden age of Victorian capitalism, madness came to represent a kind of death of the self in the midst of life. To be mad implied a moral corruption – an 1853 article in the Times conceded *in strictness, we are all mad when we give way to passion, to prejudice, to vice, to vanity.* To Alfred, for whom morality was everything, this was a truly terrifying prospect – one that could have raised thoughts of suicide.

It is likely that his diminished sense of self-esteem was accentuated by his feelings of loneliness. He had never really recovered from the deaths of his wife and son all those years ago. His wish had always been for a wife who *in her purity and capacity for 'sweet ordering'*, as the influential Victorian critic and essayist John Ruskin memorably put it, *the angel in the house was to sanctify the home as a refuge for her menfolk from the trouble of public life.* When he and Louie were married, they had looked forward to being surrounded by a host of children and later, grandchildren, as his mother had done in Hambleden. He had been one of thirteen siblings, his eldest brother had had a family of twelve (by three wives, incidentally), brother George had seven children, brother Spencer had ten; the Queen herself had had nine children – large families were seen as a source of individual and collective good, an outward sign of success. But not, sadly, for Alfred. His marriage had lasted only three years, and his son, dearest Eddy, had been only twenty-four when he died. One may imagine the remorse he suffered when he looked back on how he had been unable to be there at their deaths. So, although his extended family was large, he felt alone.

The question remains, though, why did he not remarry? Two of his older brothers had married twice, and had large families. He had been only thirty-five when his wife had died; he was wealthy, from a good family with impeccable connections, and was a well-respected and upwardly mobile officer in the Royal Navy – a good catch. His social circle was wide, and he must have had many opportunities to form a relationship with an eligible woman (perhaps a widow) of the right social standing during his career, someone to help him in the complex ordering and management of his life, someone with whom to share his grand social life. Yet, in an age in which it was an established truth – one endorsed by the medical profession, the Church, and by the population at large - that all men were possessed of a naturally strong sexual appetite, it is perhaps unusual that he volunteered for a celibate life. He seemed to have valued moral, physical and sexual reserve, and their associated notions of self-control, asceticism, purpose and industry over the comforts that a wife might have given him.

A lifetime at sea, in positions of command with no-one to confide in or even talk to, took its toll. Things that needed to be said in the Navy were said briefly and bluntly. In confined spaces emotions had to be suppressed; great achievements and terrible horrors were alike understated. Living up to the image of the British sailor as being a man of few words, grimly determined and able to make the best of a hard job, might have been reassuring in times of crisis, but in a peacetime retirement made making normal social conversation difficult. He had no one close enough to be his confidant; brothers and sisters, nephews and nieces simply do not fill the gap.

Perhaps Alfred might have mitigated his loneliness if he had been able to sink comfortably back into the civilian society he had known most of his life and where he felt he belonged – that of Hambleden. But that was not to be. On retirement, he did move back to Hambleden Cottage, still occupied by his elderly sister Harriet Amelia (Emily), and re-entered village life. But life in Hambleden came to an end in 1885 with the death of sister Emily. The Parish Magazine records….

> *The death of our dear and respected friend, Miss Ryder, took many of us by surprise. Her last illness was short, and, indeed, it was considered that she might recover from it until very shortly before her death. We were all aware that she had been for some time growing feeble, but nevertheless, hoped that her life might have been spared to us a little longer. Her long connection with the Parish had lasted for nearly half a century, and it is difficult to fancy Hambleden and Hambleden Church without her. Her quiet, peaceable life was spent amongst us 'doing good' both by deed and example. By her death we have all lost a good friend and neighbour, and many of our poor people will miss her kind help and sympathy exceedingly.*
>
> *But what helps to intensify our loss is that Hambleden Cottage will no longer be tenanted by the kind friends who have been connected with it for so many years. The honoured name of 'Ryder' is a household word in this Parish, and although it will never be forgotten, it will not henceforth be so conspicuously before us, connected with every good work, as it has been. The breaking up, in a measure, of old associations, naturally brings sadness, but we hope, nevertheless, that we shall from time to time see something of our old friends in the future, though it cannot be as frequently as it has been in the past.'[163]*

Alfred's last act in the village was to write to the new rector, Charles Wetherall….

> *I understand that it is your wish to enlarge the school chapel at Skirmett. If you carry out this idea of having a **substantial**[164] structure, and the work is commenced before July 1st, 1886, I shall be happy to guarantee a subscription from our family*

of £50, in memory of Miss Emily Ryder, who had been a resident for 47 years, and took great interest in the welfare of Skirmett.'[165],[166]

It was not, though, the last time Alfred visited the village. That was in November 1887 to attend the wedding of his second cousin, John Ryder (later to become the 5th Earl of Harrowby) to Miss Mabel Smith, WHS's eldest daughter....

> *There were ten bridesmaids and one little page of three years old – Jack Codrington – who performed his duties splendidly, although he fell over full length in the Chancel, and had to be restored to a perpendicular position by the chief bridesmaid who walked behind him!*
>
> *The pair departed for Reading station on their way to Sandon Hall, the seat of the Earl of Harrowby, uncle of the bridegroom, where they will spend the first part of their honeymoon.*[167]

So, although somewhat tenuously, Alfred became related to his friend and political superior, WHS. Mabel became Countess of Harrowby and was named Dame Commander of the Order of the British Empire (DBE) in 1919. She and her husband died within 3 days of each other in 1956.

In 1882 his uncle, Henry March-Phillipps had left Alfred the rather grand Wellswood House in Torquay. Until the death of Emily, he had divided his time between Devon and Hambleden, but after her death he gave up the lease on the family house in Hambleden and moved completely to the west country. For some reason he denied himself the chance of living out his days in his Hambleden family home – a home he had loved for nearly half a century, in which a warm welcome had always awaited him when he had returned from the sea, in a village that held him in enormous esteem (second only to WHS), and in the graveyard of which rested his son, mother and sister. Instead he chose Wellswood which he shared with his elder sister Anna (who would die there in 1893), his aunt and niece. After the family moved from Hambleden, this became the family home, often visited by his two elderly bachelor brothers,

William and Richard. It was a home he came to love – he referred to it as 'beautiful', and was comfortably looked after by five women servants, a butler and an indoor 'lad'. In the garden he employed a gardener, two men and another 'lad'. He added a library and a morning room, and made an unused bedroom habitable so that he might entertain guests.

But it was not Hambleden, and becoming part of a new community, as we all know, can be difficult. Nonetheless, his obituary in the Western Morning News noted….

> *that he would be much missed in Torquay where he took considerable interest in benevolent works and did a great deal to promote them by giving time and money. He was especially prominent in supporting the jubilee effort for the extension of the School of Science and Art, towards the funds of which he contributed £50 only about a fortnight since'.*[168]

Trewman's Exeter Flying Post[169] commented on his membership of the Torquay Science and Art Schools, and his *generous initiative and untiring energy* in funding improvements and developments.

Alfred, in retirement, was able to devote most of his energies to the cause with which he had been involved, off and on, during his active service - an Evangelical mission to rescue 'fallen women' – the complete antithesis of his ideal of the 'angel in the house'. To be clear, this was not some sort of perverted crusade on Alfred's part; on the contrary, questions about population growth, illegitimacy, prostitution – the range of problems brought into focus by the growth of densely-crowded urban society – were high on the Victorian political agenda. The provision of homes and reformatories for these unfortunate souls was a popular charitable activity involving large numbers of middle-class people, especially women, in fund raising and personal visits.

Alfred was no stranger to prostitution. It was an ubiquitous and visible feature of London life – in 1862 it was estimated that there were 80,000 prostitutes in the County of London. Although this is probably an exaggerated number as it would have meant that 20% of all women between the ages of fifteen and fifty in London were prostitutes, it was likely to have been based on a desire to scaremonger. However, if the figure was only 8,000, this would have meant in the region of one woman in fifty was 'on the game' – still an astonishing number.

Prostitution was so flagrant and unavoidable in the Haymarket and surrounding streets – including Pall Mall, where his two brothers lived[170] – that Dostoyevsky, on his one visit to London in 1862, was driven to record ….

> 'Here there are old women, here there are beauties at the sight of which makes you stop in amazement.' [171]

It is interesting he mentions 'beauties' as the prostitutes on the whole were elegantly and neatly dressed, with very few sporting make-up, quite unlike the cartoons of the day.

Nearly twenty years later, a report on the subject to the House of Lords stated:

> From 3 o'clock in the afternoon, it is impossible for any respectable woman to walk from the top of the Haymarket to Wellington Street, Strand. From 3 or 4 o'clock in the afternoon, Villiers Street and Charing Cross Station, and the Strand, are crowded with prostitutes, who are openly soliciting prostitution in broad daylight. At half past 12 at night, when 20,000 people were on the streets as theatres and pubs closed their doors, a calculation was made a short time ago that there were 500 prostitutes between Piccadilly Circus and the bottom of Waterloo Place.[172]

In actuality, the seldom-voiced truth was that as daughters, employees or servants, young women were subject to male authority; as whores they enjoyed economic and personal independence. In comparison to other occupations, prostitution was a leisured and profitable trade, by which women improved their circumstances, helped to educate siblings and often saved enough to open a shop or lodging house. Records indicate that prostitutes could earn between £4 and an extremely lucrative £35 a week.

As a naval officer, Alfred could hardly have failed to notice the activities of his crew when in port. Venereal disease was one of the most common sailor's diseases, and its incidence was closely linked to the number of prostitutes ashore and the ease with which women could be brought on board – it was not until 1869 that women were excluded from warships without express consent. A memoir in 1881, attributed to Alfred, described the following:

> *The ship filled with prostitutes at every port, by permission of the commanding officer. Not many years ago (it was since 1840) the captain of a frigate in a West Indian port (Barbados) gave an order to the first lieutenant that every man and boy was to have a black woman on board, and the order was carried out; but that was, at that date, an exceptional case.*[173]

Following the Contagious Diseases Acts of 1864 which sought to safeguard the 'protectors of the nation' - soldiers and sailors - from venereal disease, suspected prostitutes could be confined in a lock hospital until they were deemed to be 'recovered'. Imagine being a woman on the streets of Portsmouth in 1866, and you happen to be in an area known to be frequented by prostitutes. A plain clothed police officer comes up to you and tells you that he is going to have to take you in because he believes you to be a prostitute. If a magistrate agrees with him, you are forced to undergo an intrusive medical examination to look for venereal diseases. You could then be incarcerated for a six-week period, although 'sentences' of six months were not uncommon. If you refused to be examined or hospitalised, you could be imprisoned, often with hard labour. Once inside, you were stripped, bathed and issued with institutional clothing. You were then subjected to a regime of two internal inspections a week with a speculum, and required to flush out your vagina with a medicated solution using a 'vaginal douche' four times a day.

No provision was made for the examination of prostitutes' clientele – the assumption was that prostitution was a necessary evil, and while men would be offended at the intrusion, the women were already so degraded that further humiliations were of no consequence. This became one of the many points of contention in a campaign to repeal the Contagious Diseases Acts – a campaign led by Josephine Butler (another cousin of Prime Minister Lord Grey) that sparked the debate over inequality between men and women, and became an early political issue that led to women organising themselves and actively campaigning for their rights.

Alfred had entered the debate in 1876 when, as Commander-in-Chief of the British Fleet in China, he pointed out the positive results of lock hospitals in Britain to the Shanghai Municipal Council, and persuaded them to open one. On his return to Britain, he joined several well-meaning organisations - the Church Penitentiary Association, the Church of England Purity Society (of which he became a trustee), and the Diocesan Home (Winchester) for the Friendless and Fallen. In 1883, under the auspices of the Church of England Purity Society, he presented a paper on *'Purity and the Prevention of the Degradation of Women and Children'* to a session of the Church Congress at Reading, a session, incidentally, from which women were excluded. He railed at the Government for the ....

> *'rise in venereal disease in military and naval hospitals, and the fall in the number of female lock ward cases, while not closing brothels nor taking girls under the age of fourteen[174] out of them.'*

It was the plight of these young girls that most exercised him:

> *'The greatest defect, however, ...lies in the inadequate protection the law affords the young. The law against seduction affords no protection to a child over 13, and neither that nor the abduction laws afford any protection against the deeper evil of prostitution, or against those who trade on the inexperience and ignorance of the young. The Common Law of most continental countries makes the debauching of minors up to 21 an indictable offence, and subjects those who harbour minors for improper purposes to heavy fines and imprisonment. This does not exist in the Common Law of England.'*

Subsequently, at his own expense, he published 500 copies of his speech and other documents in a 120-page book, for sale for a shilling.

Into the debate stepped one William Thomas Stead[175], editor of the Pall Mall Gazette[176]. In July, 1885, in the wake of Josephine Butler's fight for the repeal of the Contagious Diseases Acts, Stead entered upon a crusade against child prostitution by publishing a series of four articles entitled *'The Maiden Tribute of Modern Babylon'*. In order to demonstrate the facility of the child prostitution industry, he arranged the 'purchase' of one Eliza Armstrong, a 13-year-old daughter of a chimney sweep. Eliza was taken to a brothel and lightly drugged to await the arrival of her purchaser, who was Stead. He entered Eliza's room and waited for her to wake from her stupor. When she came to, Eliza screamed. Stead quickly left the room, and Eliza was taken care of by the Salvationist Army.

In the meantime, Stead wrote his story.

His first instalment was trailed with a warning guaranteed to make the Pall Mall Gazette sell out. Copies changed hands for 20 times their face value and the office was besieged by 10,000 members of the public. The popularity of the articles was so great that the Gazette's supply of paper ran out and had to be replenished with supplies from the rival Globe.

Stead revealed to a respectable readership a criminal underworld of stinking brothels, a cross-channel trade in girls to the continent, drugs and padded chambers, where upper-class paedophiles could revel 'in the cries of an immature child'. For his successful demonstration of the ease and existence of the 'white slave trade', he was rewarded with a conviction for the abduction of Eliza with a three-month sentence on the technical grounds that he had failed to first secure permission for the 'purchase' from the girl's father. Nonetheless, Stead is credited with being the first investigative journalist creating a news event rather than just reporting it.

By this time, public opinion had caused the Contagious Diseases Acts to be suspended[177], a move with which Alfred did not totally agree – he had seen at first hand the havoc that sexually transmitted diseases could wreak on a ship's crew and had supported the cause of lock hospitals. However, the lock hospital system was plainly not working – an 1882 survey estimated that there were only 402 beds for female patients in all the voluntary lock hospitals in the whole of Great Britain, and female venereal patients generally had to resort to workhouse infirmaries.

At the same time, the Purity movement was becoming much criticised because of its

> 'fatuous belief that you can oblige human beings to be moral by force, and in so doing that you may in some way promote social purity'[178].

Moreover, its attempts to suppress what it considered to be indecent literature (including information on birth control), and the supposedly promiscuous entertainment[179] provided by the music halls were falling on deaf ears, so the focus of Alfred's attention became the stricter enforcement of laws against brothels, especially with regard to young girls.

He campaigned for more refuges to be established for 'fallen women'. He also encouraged

> 'organising local bodies of leading citizens into Vigilance Committees to induce School Boards and Magistrates to carry out the laws for the protection of children; such Committees to meet at least monthly, with a beadle appointed and paid by the Committee to bring cases before the Magistrates.'

And that......

> '.... steps should be taken by the inhabitants of every town to establish an Industrial School near at hand for such brothel girls'[180]

And he practised what he preached. In 1864 he had proposed the establishment of a home for penitent 'fallen' women in Basingstoke, to provide them with *the chance of recovering the character they had lost before God and society*. In 1874 purpose-built premises[181] were constructed to accommodate 48 young women, who would stay for two years, learn needlework, laundry, dairy work, and cooking, and so become good wives and mothers. Further refuges were established in Southsea, Gosport,

Southampton, Guildford and Aldershot. In 1885 Alfred persuaded the Bishop of Winchester to lend his official support by dedicating the chapel at Basingstoke, and the following year he had printed and distributed at his own expense, a lengthy speech by the Bishop of Peterborough in support of the motion….

> *That this meeting is of opinion that a temporary refuge, to which fallen women may have ready access, but without any pledge to make a lengthened stay, is urgently needed in this town and neighbourhood, and it heartily commends the refuge in the Newarke[182], established by the Leicester Ruridecanal Church of England Purity Society, and under the management of the Wantage Sisterhood, to the confidence and support of the town and county.*

Alfred signed himself *A Treasurer of the Church Penitentiary Association, a Trustee of the Church of England Purity Society, and of the Diocesan Home (Winchester) for the Friendless and Fallen* which was a good summary of where his interest lay.

In the summer of 1885, Alfred widened his attacks on immorality by addressing the troubled subject of nude artists' models. His views on the subject, as in all things, were driven by his religious beliefs – that the nude, possibly the most persistent and problematic subject in the history of human art - was associated with sensual gratification and pagan practices. The temptation of sexual indulgence was to him a conflict between the highest part of human nature, the soul, and the lowest, the body with its animal appetites. We have noted how the Times had linked vice and madness. The body was thus seen to be in constant need of surveillance as a guard against physical temptation. Beyond the emphasis on physical self-control, he and other purists, as we have seen, made it their concern to invigilate those sections of society they deemed most vulnerable and susceptible to sexual exploitation – working class women, particularly prostitutes and young people of all classes. Female artists' models also came within the orbit of his Evangelical scrutiny, since he equated modelling with involuntary, and perhaps not so involuntary, prostitution. Nevertheless, the uncertain status of both prostitutes and models caused him to believe that they were both in danger of being victimised by depraved men.

His views may have been formed by his attendance at the Paris Exhibition of 1866 and his period in Paris as the Naval Attaché in 1869. He had always been interested in art, and was an enthusiastic water colourist, though in perhaps a naïve and cartoon-like style, so when he was appointed to Paris he took advantage of being in the centre of European art by visiting as many galleries as he had time for. Two paintings in particular shocked him, both by Manet – 'Déjeuner sur l'herbe'[183] and 'Olympia'.[184]

When 'Déjeuner sur l'herbe' was rejected by the official Salon in 1863, its appearance in the hastily organised Salon de Refusés ensured that its notoriety was even greater. In Déjeuner, the nude figure was removed from the realm of allegory, religious or otherwise, and placed, life size, into a contemporary context. The painting depicts the juxtaposition of a female nude and a scantily dressed female bather in the background, on a picnic with two fully dressed men in a rural setting. The painting sparked public notoriety and stirred up controversy - it was interpreted as depicting rampant prostitution in the Bois de Boulogne – an activity that was common knowledge but considered a taboo subject for a painting.

'Olympia' (1865) is a painting of a reclining nude woman, attended by a maid and a black cat, gazing mysteriously at the viewer. Why were visitors to the Paris gallery, already quite familiar with art featuring the naked body, so outraged by the painting that the gallery was forced to hire two policemen to protect the canvas? Because art lovers were only accustomed to seeing female nudes in the guise of nymphs or goddesses, the objections to 'Olympia' had more to do with the realism of the subject matter than the fact that the model was nude. While Olympia's pose had classic precedents, the subject of the painting represented a prostitute; in the painting, the maid offers the courtesan a bouquet of flowers, presumably a gift from a client, not the sort of scene previously depicted in the art of the era.

Up to 1877, although the demand for female models was increasing, portrayal of the nude in London's Royal Academy and elsewhere in Britain, was very much based on classical lines, using archaeological reconstruction as a pretext, with painters setting about replicating the poses of antique statues. However, in that year the Academy exhibited Alma-Tadema's 'A Sculpture's Model'[185], in which, although depicted in the classic form, the model was thought to be too lifelike, conjuring up all the decadence of Rome and contemporary French art.

The debate over 'A Sculptor's Model' started as being confined to academic circles, but when it was exhibited in the Liverpool Autumn Exhibition in September 1878, it became the focus of public controversy. A letter to the Liverpool Daily Post expressed disgust at the painting, arguing that such works were best confined to the studio or dissecting room, but elsewhere in society they were evil.

It is possible that the debate would not have ignited had the appearance of 'A Sculptor's Model' not coincided with the launch of Josephine Butler's campaign to repeal the Contagious Diseases Acts. The Purity movement, seeking to cleanse society of all manifestations of immorality, politicised the nude by making it a matter of public debate. The art establishment responded by arguing that a society that hides the body is hypocritical in its morals and culture, and it was essential that works like 'A Sculptor's Model' be exhibited in public in order to promote respect for womanhood by encouraging them to seek to emulate the classical form rather than distorting their figures through tight-lacing and scandalous society dresses. For both sides, female purity was set up as a national paradigm which must be protected against 'degenerate' foreign influences.

It was inevitable that the furore surrounding 'A Sculptors Model' would inaugurate a change in the way artists treated the nude, and by the early 1880s a younger generation of painters was exhibiting works which marked a shift towards the sensational realism.

Purity protests took the form of letters in the press from men and women drawing attention to the plight of young female models and the 'iniquitous' practice followed by some art schools of allowing men and women to study the model together. One such correspondent was Alfred, writing in 1885 under the pseudonym of 'XYZ'. He made it abundantly clear that he was a staunch opponent of the life class, and encouraged the public to boycott galleries displaying nude works. He collated a selection of letters to *The Times* into a pamphlet for wider circulation. He was the driving force behind a paper delivered to Portsmouth Church Congress in which it was argued that life study was 'unwomanly' and violated Christian principles, that female artists, trained at public expense, assisted in the degradation of their sex. Such widespread purity agitation gave rise to a general anxiety that female nudes, female models and female students of art were yet further symptoms of a decline in national morals. For Alfred and the purists, the issue was all about guarding female virtue, while his opponents charged him with prudery and ignorance. Alfred could not let it rest – he sought advice from his barrister brothers as to whether he could prosecute the Academy for exhibiting pictures of naked women which, as it turned out, proved fruitless.

Just as the debate over 'A Sculptors Model' seemed to be dying down, Théodore Roussel's 'The Reading Girl'[186] was exhibited at the New English Art Club in 1887, in opposition to the Royal Academy. Its frank nudity is not presented as a classical Venus, but rather as a robust and healthy young woman, with a taste for current fashion. The discarded kimono, the model's elegant hairstyle and the folding campaign chair all contributed to the controversy. The critic for the Spectator wrote:

> *'Our imagination fails to conceive any adequate reason for a picture of this sort. It is realism of the worst kind, the artist's eye seeing only the vulgar outside of his model, and reproducing that callously and brutally. No human being, we should imagine, could take any pleasure in such a picture as this; it is a degradation of Art'*[187].

The exhibiting of this painting came as a blow to Alfred; perhaps for the first time he came to realise that the social purity movement was ineffective in banning the nude from public exhibition, or in regulating the number of female models and female students in art schools. The weight of common-sense opinion emphasised the professionalism and morality of both artist and model in the face of the apparent uninformed misconceptions of the purists. Added to which the Archbishop of Canterbury cautioned that the Church of England had no right to intrude in matters beyond its jurisdiction.........and so the case was lost.

The controversy over the exhibition of 'scandalous' paintings must be seen in the context of British art of the period, which emphasised Romanticism in works by such as Constable and Turner. It was fashionable to draw on literary and biblical themes, most famously in the Pre-Raphaelite movement with artists such as Hunt[188], Rosetti and Millais with their ultra-realistic and minutely detailed works. The feature of academic and portrait painting of the age was that it was seldom at war with established society; cultural bohemianism had very little impact on wider society, and many artists became extremely successful – no freezing garrets for them – and the president of the Royal Academy from 1878, Sir Frederick Leighton, was the first (and, so far, only) painter to receive a peerage.[189]

The high walls of the permissible of course disguised hypocrisy on a grand scale. And nowhere was this more apparent than in the corpulent figure of the idle, pleasure-loving Prince of Wales, the future Edward VII, himself involved in several public scandals. His first scandal was the Mordaunt case of 1870, in which the Prince was cited as a co-respondent in a divorce case, and was forced to swear he had not committed adultery. Few believed him. In the spring of 1871, he fathered a child by Lady Susan Vane – and then washed his hands of her. There were strong rumours later that year of an alliance with a Parisian courtesan............and so the procession of mistresses and alleged bastards continued throughout the 1870s. Lily Langtry, the actress who became the Prince's most celebrated mistress met him in 1877. The Prince's name was further blackened when, again, he was cited as co-respondent when Lily's husband sought to divorce her.

The Prince's sexual proclivities were only part of the problem. His self-indulgent life, devoted to the pursuit of pleasure – shooting, house parties, travelling, yachting – set a poor example to a society flirting with republicanism, in which an increasingly educated and politically-aware working class were alert to inequalities. And what made it all seem so much worse to someone as upright as Alfred was the fact that the Prince had been married since 1863, and had six children by the time of the Vane affair. That someone should squander life with a wife and six children was unforgivable to Alfred, who had longed for such a family.

Neither was Alfred happy about what was happening in the Empire. His career in the navy had been spent defending the Empire in one way or another, almost continually under the intensely patriotic Lord Palmerston who, between 1830 and 1865, had dominated British politics. His principal aim had been to advance the national interests of England. His patriotism and love of the established order were legendary:

> *A Frenchman, thinking to be highly complimentary, said to Palmerston: 'If I were not a Frenchman, I should wish to be an Englishman'; to which he coolly replied: 'If I were not an Englishman, I should wish to be an Englishman.*[190]

> *The landed interest is the great foundation upon which rest the fabric of society, and that of the country. I mean no disparagement to manufactures and commerce; I know how essential they are to the happiness and prosperity of the country, and how much they add even to the value of the land. But the land of the country is the country itself, and the owner of the land has the deepest and most permanent interest in its well-being; tied down to the soil, he must share the fortunes of his country, whether in its greatness or its fall.*[191]

Stirring stuff, which exerted a great influence on an ambitious naval officer – especially as his brother in law, Sir George Grey, had served in Palmerston's cabinet. In 1884, Alfred, like the rest of the nation, could only watch askance as prime minister Gladstone dithered in sending Charles Gordon to Sudan to rescue British soldiers and civilians caught up in a Dervish revolt. He then dithered even more in sending a relief column to rescue him when things started to go horribly wrong. The column arrived in Khartoum two days after Gordon had been killed.

Nothing could be more different from Palmerston's 1850 speech. Following disasters in South Africa at Isandlwana and Majuba Hill, this was the third colonial reversal in the space of six years. On learning of it in February 1885, Queen Victoria's outrage echoed the popular mood. *The news from Khartoum,* she telegraphed Gladstone, *are* (stet) *frightful, and to think that all this might have been prevented and many precious lives saved by earlier action is too frightful.'*

The Times thundered

> *the mingled feelings of dismay, consternation and indignant disgust universally evoked by this lamentable result of a long course of disregard of the elementary maxims of statesmanship......a long series of blunders illuminated by the lightning flash of failure.........everything had been done that could add to the risks of defeat.*[192]

Gordon became an instant imperial martyr; the fact that he was a loner, a strange, complex religiously obsessed character – he was portrayed as a warrior saint, not exactly the typical Victorian soldier - and one who had disobeyed his instructions, was overlooked. The masses were absurdly proud of their country as a great imperial and military power (it was certainly the former; the latter, as we've seen, was debateable) – a sentiment contained in the music-hall song of 1878:

> *We don't want to fight but by Jingo if we do*
> *We've got the ships, we've got the men, we've got the money too.*

The public demanded retribution to show the Dervishes who was in charge. Unfortunately for British public opinion, the Dervishes were, and a huge dent was placed in British self-confidence, not least in Wellswood House, Torquay. Alfred was not to know that it would take over a decade for Gordon's death to be avenged.[193] He could only wonder what Sir George Grey and Palmerston would have done.

The Gordon incident brought home the limitations of the Navy in the expanding empire. Moreover, new nations had begun to seek naval power, and British complacency was shaken. In 1884, the aforementioned W T

Stead published a series of articles entitled *'The Truth about the Navy'* in which he revealed how the Navy was suffering for lack of money, and could not be guaranteed to defend the empire. Alfred could see that the vulnerability of the empire meant that starvation was a more important threat to Britain than invasion, but again, he was not to see the increase in naval estimates, the orgy of spending and shipbuilding culminating in the Naval Defence Act of 1889 which formally confirmed the 'two-power standard' by which Britain's navy should be at least equal to the sum of those of the next two naval powers – France and Russia.

One question that Stead posed was *Is it or is it not true that both the French and Italian navies* (note no mention of Germany) *are armed with heavier guns of greater precision and more convenient for handling than are our own ships?* Sadly, this question was never answered satisfactorily, for in 1914 it was clear that British gunners were underprepared for combat and were badly let down by their fire control systems. At the Battle of Jutland in 1916, just 3 per cent of British shells hit their targets! Not only were shells poorly aimed, but many which did achieve hits failed to explode or to inflict significant damage. Fuses were unreliable and often caused premature detonation. It seems the Admiralty had answered Stead's question with quantity of ships rather than quality of gunnery.

It may have been true that the national standard of living and quality of life had improved markedly across the nineteenth century – celebrated with vast outpourings of public enthusiasm across the nation on the occasion of the Queen's golden jubilee on 20 June 1887, the precise day that she had first mounted the throne. It was the celebration of Queen Victoria's unrivalled position as the doyenne of European royalty; it provided the opportunity for the crafting of a structured and self-satisfied national narrative, extolling half a century of remarkable progress, politically, socially, economically and culturally, not only for domestic consumption but internationally as well. The royal heads of Europe, Indian princes, dignitaries and representatives from all corners of the Empire converged on London. Even the Hawaiian queen, Liliuokalani attended. West End shopkeepers adorned their windows in red, white and blue; royal standards and Union Jacks, festoons of flowers and coloured garlands could be seen hanging from every sombre office edifice.

In Hambleden, plans were laid for the event:

> *The subjects of the Queen of England* (stet) *have much cause for thankfulness when they consider the blessings vouchsafed to this country and to our colonies during the past 50 yrs. Undoubtedly, it has been the best reign that England has ever known.*

> *It has been decided to celebrate the Jubilee in the parish by a day of public rejoicing. If Hambleden people will show that they can keep a <u>good, sober, sensible</u> holiday, without any way abusing it, they will offer a tribute to the Queen, that they are rightly called her <u>worthy and dutiful</u> subjects!* (original emphasis)

However, the mood of national self-congratulation was not universally shared. Victoria found herself at the head of a divided, troubled nation – in fact she heard a strange noise when she opened the People's Palace in the Mile End Road – 'booing' she believed it to be called. Prime Minister Salisbury assured her that the booers were *'probably socialists and the worst Irish.'* Nonetheless, the celebrations took place in a period of social restlessness.

The jubilee did nothing to eliminate the differences in society, the inequality between rich and poor, the falling food prices that created rural unemployment. Even in Hambleden, the economic depression was felt, causing the Rector to comment on…

> *a well-attended meeting in Hambleden recruiting for the Agricultural Workers Union with promises of higher wages*

and he….

> *urged any man before he joined to consider his lot – what he gets free on top of his wages – free cottage, harvest money, free wood, cheap coal, cheap beer. If he has grievances, he should address them to his master in the first instance, with proof.'* [194]

Alfred, of course, was aware of such rumblings – he read the Parish Magazine every month, and was alarmed when he heard about the disturbance in Trafalgar Square in February 1886 when a demonstration against unemployment[195] got out of hand; the Carlton Club was stoned and shops in Pall Mall and Piccadilly were looted. Further trouble erupted in November 1887 with another huge demonstration in the Square on what became known as 'Bloody Sunday'. As with the first demonstration, the protesters were not part of a mass movement; they had no wish to overthrow the established order - they simply wanted their fair share of the steadily increasing national prosperity. Britain in the 1880s had become an 'us and them' society[196], and London, in particular, had become the poverty capital of Britain. Then, as now, it was a magnet for the unemployed, the dispossessed and for refugees. As the largest, most opulent, city in the world it attracted immigrants from the colonies and poorer parts of Europe. There was a large Irish community, a sizable Jewish community – refugees from Russia and Poland fleeing the pogroms that followed the assassination of Tsar Alexander in 1881 - and small communities of Chinese and South Asians. Then, as now, housing was the problem, slums developed and politicians were aware of how society was being eroded and had to be protected. In 1888, it is estimated that between two hundred and six hundred people were sleeping in Trafalgar Square, less than a quarter of a mile from the Ryder's residence in Pall Mall.

Consequently, on Bloody Sunday, both the infantry and cavalry were standing by. An eye-witness described….

> no one who saw it will ever forget the strange and indeed terrible sight of that grey winter day, the vast, sombre-coloured crowd, the brief but fierce struggle at the corner of the Strand, and the river of steel and scarlet that moved slowly through the dusky swaying masses when two squadrons of Life Guards were summoned from Whitehall.' [197]

Although they were not ordered to draw their swords, nor the infantry ordered to open fire, violent clashes took place; 400 people were arrested and 75 badly injured, including many police, two policemen being stabbed and one protester bayoneted. Among those arrested was one Mary Ann 'Polly' Nichols, who tragically, on 31 August 1888, would become the first victim of Jack the Ripper.

The streets around Trafalgar Square became battlegrounds; windows were smashed, curbs torn up. In the fighting, many rioters fell under the hooves of police horses. The soldiers, who a few months before were conducting a little old lady in a bonnet through a pageant of imperialist patriotism, were now turned against the people of London. For local residents (including William and Richard Ryder) it was all extremely frightening. They could still remember Peterloo.

Underpinning everything Alfred did in his life was his Christian faith – the Christian Herald described him as *'an earnest Churchman'*[198]. His family were steeped in religion - he was the son of a bishop, sister Sophia became a nun, brothers Henry and George became Roman Catholic priests, brother Thomas was Registrar of the Manchester Diocese. Perhaps Alfred himself should have taken holy orders; as it is, he tried to be guided by his principles throughout his naval career – which we can imagine could not always have been easy. One may, perhaps, think that he would have had his faith to fall back on when other things in his life were going awry, but that assumption rather misreads the religious climate in Britain of the 1880s. Whereas the 1830s and the 1840s were dominated by the controversy surrounding the Oxford Movement, a debate that had had the power to divide the entire literate nation, the most important intellectual question of the late nineteenth century was sparked by the publication of Charles Darwin's *'On the Origin of Species'* in 1859, and *'The Descent of Man'* in 1871. Darwin, however, was simply the best known of the collection of scientists[199] who defined what Richard Holmes[200] has called 'the age of wonder'. The voyage of the Beagle, often lonely and perilous, is the defining metaphor of Romantic science.

The age of wonder included men and women who introduced new ways of thinking, about the earth, about humankind, and about scientific approaches to understanding the material world. Pioneers included

Humphry Davy, Michael Faraday, Charles Babbage, John Herschel, Mary Somerville and Charles Lyell; what a time to be alive!

With the growing knowledge of geology and astronomy, and the recognition of 'deep sky'[201] and 'deep time',[202]fewer and fewer men or women of education can have believed in a literal, Biblical, six days of creation. But until Darwin, science had yet to produce its own theory of creation. That is why *On the Origin of Species* appeared so devastating when it was published. It was not that it reduced the six days of Biblical creation to a myth: this had already been done by Lyell[203] and other geologists. What it demonstrated was that there was no need for divine creation at all. There was no divine creation of species, no miraculous invention of butterflies' wings or cats' eyes or birds' song. The process of evolution by 'natural selection' replaced any need for 'intelligent design' in nature. Darwin had indeed written a new Book of Genesis. Those raised on a strict literalistic belief in the Bible read Darwin and the others and experienced an internal crisis of faith – and Alfred was no exception. For he was also a scientist in a small way – his obituary in the Hampshire Telegraph noted that he was *an officer of considerable scientific attainments*[204]. He had written several technical papers for the Navy, including *Methods of ascertaining the distance from ships at sea*, *A treatise on economy of fuel: showing how it may be attained on board men-of-war steamers*, *Heads of enquiry into the state and condition of lighthouses*. These papers were scrupulously researched, and included the detailed tables that had become Alfred's trademark. He understood the power of scientific evidence, so it is not surprising that by the end of his life, doubt was triumphing over faith, and that his religion was not strong enough to keep his depression at bay. Indeed, his crisis in faith was a large part of his depression.

The road away from religious belief is long and tortuous; conversion is not immediate. As Alfred began to realise who he was and who he wasn't, he became conscious that the place in which his supposed religious belief dwelt had long been empty. His belief had degenerated; it no longer had any underpinning. The leaning wall would fall at the touch of a finger.

What perhaps was the final straw, that touch of the finger, was the Bradlaugh case. Originally elected as Liberal MP for Northampton in 1880, Charles Bradlaugh refused to swear the required parliamentary oath of allegiance on the grounds that he was both an atheist and a republican. He was duly expelled from the Commons and his seat was declared vacant; he would be expelled several more times after winning a series of by-elections. Eventually, in 1886, he was allowed to take his seat, and, as Alfred and his brothers were walking beside the Thames in April 1888, the Oaths Act was going through Parliament which would allow the Parliamentary oath of allegiance taken to the Sovereign to be solemnly affirmed rather than sworn to God.[205]

To Alfred and others, this demonstrated the final triumph of secularism, the final degradation of the public realm. The Church could no longer call itself the moral arbiter of society. The world that his father and his family had spent their lives moulding was over. He found himself in a place that simply made no sense.

Did he fall or did he jump? No-one will ever know. It could have been that the swell of the river caused him to lose his balance on the jetty, and topple in. However, it seems reasonable to accept that he was likely to have harboured suicidal tendencies, even though he knew that suicide was a sin and a crime. It is possible that his faith had been so dissipated that he may well not have cared. But whether his depression was sufficient to tip him over the edge…………...?

O Thou, from Whom all goodness flows,
I lift my soul to Thee
In all my sorrows, conflicts, woes,
Good Lord, remember me.

If on my aching burdened heart
My sins lie heavily,
(Thy pardon grant, Thy peace impart;
Good Lord, remember me.

If trials sore obstruct my way,
And ills I cannot flee,
Then let my strength be as my day;
Good Lord, remember me.

If worn with pain, disease, and grief,
(This feeble frame should be,
Grant patience, rest, and kind relief;
Good Lord, remember me.

And oh, when in the hour of death
I bow to Thy Decree,
Jesu, receive my parting breath:
Good Lord, remember me. Amen.

Hymn 140, as it appears in
Hymns Ancient and Modern (1867)

Acknowledgements

I am not a historian, and this is not a history – a catalogue of dates and events. But as all history is a story, so this is a story; a story about people, and one person in particular, his life and the personalities and events and that shaped it. Naturally, I have stuck to the facts whenever possible. Perhaps I should caution the reader that there are two kind of facts – facts of the past (the Battle of Hastings was fought in 1066) and facts of the present. A fact of the present is something I've interpreted to be a fact. As the historian EH Carr once said, *Facts are like fish on the fishmonger's slab. The historian collects them, takes them home and cooks and serves them.* To continue his analogy, the recipes I have used to prepare my fish have often been taken from the books of genuine scholars.

But whether history or story, fact or fable, this book is a homage to the place I love more than I can say, and to one of its most illustrious residents.

A miracle of the history of Hambleden is that the Parish Magazines from 1871 onwards are still available. They provide a wonderful record of what life was like and what issues were important from that time, and I have made frequent refences to them throughout these pages by a simple date as a footnote. I was privileged to have been granted access to these very fragile and important documents, for which I am so grateful to Mrs Jean Keene of Colstrope.

I have also drawn freely from the wonderful collation of Alfred's letters to his son *Letters to Eddy*, and from the online Ryder family archives https://ryderarchives.weebly.com. For granting permission to do this and for writing a few introductory comments, I am grateful to Alfred's great-great-nephew, Lisle Ryder.

I am indebted to Commander Mike Mason for advising me on elements of naval history and maritime strategy. If I have made errors, it is because I didn't listen to him!

Details of the risky business of childbirth in the early nineteenth century, and of tuberculosis, were provided by Dr Gerry Jarvis.

Others who have freely offered their advice are Ken Cugnoni and Maria Spink. For me, writing a book is a team effort, and their input has been invaluable.

At its most joyous, writing a book is living a parallel life, so I am also grateful to my wife, Jo, for keeping me grounded in the rather unhappy twenty first century when I was tempted to take flight into the nineteenth, a foreign country where all seemed nostalgically abundant – peace, prosperity, purpose and plenty. She took the photograph that comprises the cover for his volume.

For purposes of conversion £1 in 1850 is the equivalent of approximately £150 today.

Timeline

1820   Born in Wells, Somerset

1833   Joined Navy – Royal Naval College, Portsmouth

1836   Father died

1838   Mother and family move to Hambleden

1839   Mate on HMS Imogene

1841   Lieutenant on HMS Belvedera

1846   Promoted to Commander

1847   Senior Officer on HMS Vixen

1848   Rescued hostages in Nicaragua; promoted to Captain.

1852   Married Louisa (Louie) Dawson

1853   Birth of son, Edward (Eddy); HMS Dauntless

1854   Crimean War

1855   Louisa died

1858   Commission on Lighthouses

1861   HMS Hero Channel Squadron

1862   Mother died; Private Secretary to the First Lord of the Admiralty

1863   Controller of the Coastguard

1864   Aide-de-camp to the Queen

1866   Promoted to Rear-Admiral

1867   2nd in Command Channel Fleet

1870   Sinking of HMS Captain; Naval Attaché Paris

1871   Franco Prussian War

1872   Promoted to Vice Admiral; Naval Attaché to the Maritime Courts of Europe

1874   C in C China Station

1875   Promoted to Admiral

1877 Eddy married Agnes Bickley; Eddy died three months later; WH Smith First Lord of the Admiralty.

1879 C in C Portsmouth

1882 Retired

1885 Promoted to the honorary rank of Admiral of the Fleet

1888 Drowned in the Thames at Vauxhall

Publications by Alfred Ryder

1846   A pamphlet on the experimental cruizes [sic] of the line of battle ships in 1845: containing the results of the trials, the method pursued to obtain them, and some suggestions on the best mode of registering the necessary observations

1846, 1854, 1858   Methods of ascertaining the distance from ships at sea

1847   Plan of a floating battery for defence of the Bermudas

1847   Practical rules for determining the course to be steered to escape from a hurricane. Deduced from the rotary theory, established by Col. Reid.

1852   A treatise on economy of fuel: showing how it may be attained on board men-of-war steamers and pointing out the considerations which should be carefully studied when engines are being ordered for steamers-of-war, mail packets, or merchant ships ...

1859   Report on Navigation Schools.

1860   A Letter on the national dangers which result from the great deterioration in the seaman of the mercantile marine ; with reasons for the adoption of an apprentice system ; addressed to his Grace the Duke of Somerset.

1863   Heads of inquiry into the state and condition of lighthouses : with explanatory notes : for the use of authorities having charge of lighthouses, and for the information of lighthouse keepers, &c..

1868   Rescue of Fallen Women. A statement containing a proposal, etc.

1872   Life-saving at sea by Cork life-belts or mattresses, &c ...

1873   Penitentiary work in the Church of England : papers prepared for discussion at the anniversary meeting of the Church Penitentiary Association, on S. Mark's day, 1873, at the request of the council.

1874 The fittings of her majesty's ship Victor Emanuel as a hospital ship during the late Ashantee campaign.

1875 The Higher Education of Naval Officers, with special reference to the report of Admiral Shadwell's Committee.

1881 A Statement prepared for the Committee of Convocation of the Province of Canterbury, Lower House, in 1879-80-1, on the alleged increase of prostitution, and the best means for the recovery of the fallen.

1884 A Paper on the purity and the Prevention of the Degradation of Women and Children.

Bibliography

Anon, *A Seaman's Life on Board a Man-of-War* (Portsmouth, Griffin & Co, 1881)

Beeler, John F, *British Naval Policy in the Gladstone-Disraeli Era, 1866-1880* (Stanford, Calif., Stanford University Press, 1997)

Best, Geoffrey, *Mid-Victorian Britain 1851-1875* (London: Fontana, 1985)

Bridge, Cyprian, *The Art of Naval Warfare* (London: Smith, Elder & Co, 1907)

Carradine, David, *Victorious Century, The United Kingdom 1800-1906* (London: Allen Lane, 2017)

Colomb, PH, *Memoirs of Admiral the Right Honourable. Sir Astley Cooper Key* (London, Methuen, 1898)

Colomb, PH, *Slave Catching in the Indian Ocean* (London, Longmans, 1873)

Davis, John, *A History of Britain 1885-1939* (Basingstoke, Macmillan, 1999)

Ferguson, Niall, *Empire* (London, Penguin, 2004)

Frankopan, Peter, *The Silk Roads* (London, Bloomsbury, 2016)

Holmes, Richard, The Age of Wonder (London: Harper Collins, 2009)

Hough, Richard, *Admirals in Collision* (London, Hamish Hamilton, 1959)

Kennedy, Paul, *The Rise and Fall of British Naval Mastery* (London, Penguin, 2017)

Kennedy, William, *Hurrah for The Life of a Sailor: Fifty Years in The Royal Navy* (London & Edinburgh, Wm. Blackwood, 1900)

Lavery, Brian, *Empire of the Seas* (London: Conway, 2012)

Napier, Charles, *The History of the Baltic campaign of 1854* (London, Richard Bentley, 1857)

Padfield, Peter, *Rule Britannia* (London: Routledge & Keegan Paul, 1981)

Parkinson, Jonathan, *The Royal Navy, China Station 1864-1941* (Kibworth Beauchamp: Matador, 2018)

Paterson, Michael, *Life in Victorian Britain* (London, Constable & Robinson, 2008)

Penrose-Fitzgerald, Charles, *Memories of the Sea* (London, Edward Arnold, 1913)

Prettejohn, Elizabeth (Ed), *After the Pre-Raphaelites* (Manchester, Manchester University Press, 1999)

Rubenstein, William D, *The World Hegemon : The British Isles 1832-1914* (London, Vintage, 2015)

Ryder, Lisle, *Letters to Eddy* (Woodbridge, Carlford Books, 2014)

Stanton, AH, *On Chiltern Slopes* (Oxford, Blackwell, 1927)

Walkowitz, Judith, *Prostitution and Victorian Society: Women, Class, and the State* (Cambridge, Cambridge University Press, 1982)

Walvin, James, *Victorian Values* (London, André Deutsch, 1987)

Wilson, Ben, *Empire of the Deep* (London: Phoenix, 2014)

Wilson, Ben, *Heyday* (London: Weidenfeld and Nicholson, 2016)

Winton, John, *Hurrah for the Life of a Sailor!* (London, Michael Joseph, 1977)

Notes

1   A Monday - the tradition of taking Monday off had been common among craft workers since at least the seventeenth century. The tradition declined during the nineteenth century.

2   If this figure is correct, it would have meant that practically half the population of Manchester and surrounding towns were present.

3   Samuel Bamford, a radical and writer. After the Massacre, he was arrested and charged with treason and sentenced to a year in Lincoln gaol.

4   Now a rather undistinguished street off the Edgeware Road.

5   The Oxford Movement was a movement of High Church members of the Church of England which eventually developed into Anglo-Catholicism. The movement, whose original devotees were mostly associated with the University of Oxford, argued for the reinstatement of some older Christian traditions of faith and their inclusion into Anglican liturgy and theology.

6   The Henley branch line and station were not opened until 1857.

7   One of the first problems she had to overcome was understanding the locals. In 1838 the word 'Hambleden' had a silent 'b'; it was pronounced 'Hummuldun' and would remain so until the level of literacy increased during the nineteenth century.

8   If you are interested in modern obstetric procedures (or even if you're not), I strongly recommend 'This is Going to Hurt' by Adam Kay : Picador 2018 – a funny, moving and important book.

9   The Spectator 4 December 1830

10 Earl Grey owned an estate of over 1,000 acres in Fallodon, Northumberland.

11 Possibly the highest percentage of the city's population as spectators to a state occasion of any event in history.

12 In a BBC poll in 2002, Nelson was voted the ninth most famous Briton, behind Winston Churchill, Isambard Kingdom Brunel, Diana, Princess of Wales, Charles Darwin, William Shakespeare, Sir Isaac Newton, Elizabeth I and John Lennon. Ninth he may be, but without him we would all be speaking French now! 'Donner une chance à la paix' does not have quite the same ring about it!

13 http://www.britishempire.co.uk/maproom/captureofslaver.htm

14 It is not known why the boat from the *Naiad* capsized. The Tiber mouth at that period was navigable only with difficulty because of the whirlpools and shoals created by the sand and debris carried downstream by the river; perhaps they played a role in the tragedy, but this is speculation.

15 Letters to Eddy : 9 December 1856

16 Letters to Eddy : 30 December 1856

17 Letters to Eddy : 7 January 1857

18 Letters to Eddy : 28 January 1857

19 P H Colomb in Navy & Army Illustrated, June 1897.

20 MP for the Northern division of Leicestershire; former High Sheriff of Leicestershire. Reportedly one of the wealthiest commoners in England.

21 Either orca or Risso's dolphin

22 Son of Earl Grey, later to become an Admiral. The 1871 census shows him living at Yewden, Hambleden

23 Jane Austen's brother, an old boy of the Royal Naval College, Portsmouth.

24 An abattis is a field fortification consisting of an obstacle formed of the branches of trees laid in a row, with the sharpened tops directed outwards, towards the enemy. The trees are usually interlaced or tied with wire.

25 Broad Arrow 5 May 1888

26 Oxford Dictionary of National Biography

27 Letters to Eddy 23 April 1861

28 Letters to Eddy 14 June 1861

29 Broad Arrow, op.cit.

30 The Art of Naval Warfare : Admiral Sir Cyprian Bridge : Smith, Elder & Co, 1907

31 Palmerston's speech on affairs in Greece : 25 June 1850 : Hansard

32 A series of laws, dating from 1651 that restricted colonial trade to England.

33 P H Colomb : Memoirs of Admiral Sir Astley Cooper Key : Methuen, 1898

34 https://www.nationalgallery.org.uk/paintings/joseph-mallord-william-turner-the-fighting-temeraire

35 Paradoxically, Britain's merchant shipbuilding was far in advance of her rivals. Brunel's Great Western (1838), Great Britain (1843) and Great Eastern (1858) were the largest and most technologically advanced ships in the world.

36 Letters to Eddy 4 October 1861

37 Memories of the Sea, Admiral Penrose Fitzgerald : Edward Arnold, London 1913

38 At Trafalgar, Nelson split his fleet in two and sailed at right angles into the French and Spanish line, seeking to split it up. The tactic - also known as

'crossing the T' - was not new but had never been used as a deliberate battle plan before.

39 South of the Serpentine, between Rotten Row and South Carriage Drive.

40 The recently reopened Temperate House at Kew is a mere 191 metres long!

41 It was constructed of 30,000 hand blown glass panes.

42 The following mainline stations were opened by 1851: London Bridge (1836), Euston (1837), Paddington (1838), Fenchurch St (1841), Waterloo (1848)

43 About 36,500 a day!

44 The building was dismantled soon after the Exhibition ended, and was re-erected in Sydenham, south London. It burned down and was destroyed in 1936.

45 Charles John Napier, The History of the Baltic campaign of 1854 : Richard Bentley : 1857

46 Napier ibid

47 Letter dated 11 May 1854

48 Alfred's brother in law, Sir George Grey, was Secretary of State for the Colonies. Henry Codrington's late father had been a hero of Trafalgar, and a knighted admiral.

49 Letters to Eddy 10 March 1856

50 The original is at Sandon Hall.

51 In 1858

52 The letters can be found at https://ryderarchives.weebly.com/letters-to-eddy.html, and are also reproduced in the wonderfully illustrated 'Letters to Eddy', copies of which can be obtained from Alfred's great, great nephew Lisle Ryder lisleryder@gmail.com

53 Possibly Alfred's secretary Thomas Royle

54 Possibly an Eagle Owl (wingspan 1.4m-1.7m)

55 Now Cobh.

56 Letters to Eddy 23 October 1856

57 The Standard 5 March 1857.

58 Alfred's youngest sibling.

59 HMS Hero was decommissioned in 1862; its successor found fame of sorts by being named on the cap-band of the seaman featured in the logo of Player's Navy Cut cigarettes.

60 My exclamation mark!

61 The first edition cost fourteen shillings – about £400 in today's money. If you can track down a first edition today, it is likely to set you back £80,000!

62 Southampton Herald 9 February 1861.

63 Letters to Eddy April 20 1861.

64 Letters to Eddy April 23 1861.

65 Cork Constitution 2 October 1861

66 Letters to Eddy; July 17 1861

67 29 July 1861

68 Letters to Eddy September 4 1861

69 Prince Albert was to die three months later – sadly, it would be a long time before the Queen would look 'well and happy' again.

70 Vice-Admiral Sir William Kennedy: Hurrah for the life of a sailor - fifty years in the Royal Navy, 1900

71 Letters to Eddy : 10 April 1862

72 Slave Catching in the Indian Ocean; PH Colomb, Longmans 1873

73 Sir Frederick Grey, Sir George Grey and the Duke of Somerset were all members of Palmerston's Cabinet. It's not what you know.............

74 It has been said that his last words were, 'Die, my dear doctor? That is the last thing I shall do!"

75 The school, now a private residence, was the 'home' of the Beatles in the film 'A Hard Day's Night'.

76 Of the 40 boys who left the school on 1871, 16 joined military bands.

77 At the time, Chancellor of the Exchequer.

78 Morning Post 22 March 1872

79 Battle of Magdala 1868

80 John F. Beeler : British Naval Policy in the Gladstone-Disraeli Era, 1866-1880 : Stanford Press, 1997.

81 Naval & Military Gazette 27 May 1868.

82 Glasgow Herald 18 September 1868

83 Letters to Eddy : 10 June 1868

84 Letters to Eddy : 7 January 1857

85 Letters to Eddy : 20 April 1861

86 Letters to Eddy : 12 June 1868

87 *Bellerophon* was named after the ship of the same name on which Napoleon finally surrendered. A verse from a popular sea shanty of the time records *Boney went a-cruisin', Away a-yeah, Aboard the Billy Ruffian, Jean Francois*

88 Letters to Eddy : 4 October 1861

89 Her commander Hugh Burgoyne, an experienced officer who had been awarded the Victoria Cross in the Crimea, was one of the very few men somehow to clamber onto the upturned hull – but he then refused to jump to the safety of the ship's launch and went down atop his ship

90 Chiders took personal responsibility for the loss of the *Captain*, and resigned.

91 After his death, a 'Ryder Memorial Prize' was established for the sub lieutenant who came first in the French exam at the Royal Naval College, Greenwich

92 Lord Palmerston is reported to have said: 'Only three people have ever really understood the Schleswig-Holstein business—the Prince Consort, who is dead—a German professor, who has gone mad—and I, who have forgotten all about it.'

93 The Suez Canal had been opened in 1869.

94 The subsequent investigation on the loss of the Captain, in the form of a court-martial, concluded that "the Captain was built in deference to public opinion expressed in Parliament and through other channels, and in opposition to views and opinions of the Controller and his Department". This conclusion is engraved upon the Memorial in the north aisle of St. Paul's Cathedral

95 Royal United Services Institute Journal, Vol 15, 1871 : The Naval Hammock—its Buoyancy and Use in Saving Life at Sea

96 The Times 26 Jan 1872

97 An officer training hulk, moored at Greenhithe, now called the Incorporated Thames Nautical Training College, part of the Merchant Navy College at Greenhithe.

98 After his death, a group of senior officers instituted a prize in his memory for *the Officer, of any rank, who passes the best examination for interpreter.*

99 Morning Post 30 May 1874

100 China's coastline alone is over 9,000 miles long; the China Sea has an area of 1.4m square miles.

101 July 1874

102 Members of both the Jardine and Matheson families represented the 'rotten' Borough of Ashburton off and on between 1841 and 1868. Members of the Ryder family represented the neighbouring equally 'rotten' borough of Tiverton, so it seems probable that the families knew each other.

103 The P&O Line itself shipped 632,000 tons of opium from Bengal to China between 1847 and 1858.

104 It is one of the ironies of British history that whereas on the one hand Britain led the crusade against the slave trade, on the other it was instrumental in establishing the world trade in narcotics. What these events had in common was that British naval mastery made them possible.

105 Shanghai, Canton (Guangzhou), Ningpo (Ningbo), Fuchow (Fuzhou), and Amoy (Xiamen)

106 Cited by Peter Frankopan : The Silk Roads : Bloomsbury : London : 2016

107 Now Wonsan, on the east coast of North Korea.

108 Tsushima Island is an island of the Japanese archipelago situated in the Korea Strait, approximately halfway between the Japanese mainland and the Korean Peninsula

109 The Russian navy tried to establish a base on the island in 1861, but the effort failed due to British intervention.

110 Port Hamilton, now Geomun-do is a small group of islands off the southern coast of the Korean Peninsula,

111 Maidenhead Railway Bridge was built in 1838, and was a thing of wonder as the two arches were the widest and flattest in the world. It is testimony to the genius of Brunel that such a bridge with such flat arches was not only built but continues to carry the Great Western Railway main line from Paddington Station to this day. In 1874, it carried two 7ft gauge tracks.

112 Finished in 1872, though the statue of Albert was not added till 1875.

113 Paddington to the Museum is about 2 miles.

114 Presented to the museum by Sir Garnet Wolseley following his victory over the Ashanti king, Kofi Kakari only five months earlier.

115 The station had been opened in 1868.

116 Only ten years old in 1874.

117 Baedeker's 1889 guide to London listed Gatti's as one of the top restaurants in the West End.

118 About 3 miles.

119 Rule Britannia, The Victorian and Edwardian Navy : Peter Padfield : Routledge and Keegan Paul, 1981

120 Quoted by Richard Hough : Admirals in Collision : Hamish Hamilton 1959

121 28 October 1875

122 A Chinese politician, general and diplomat

123 Sir Thomas Wade, British Minister to China.

124 A covered litter for one passenger, consisting of a large box carried on two horizontal poles by four or six bearers.

125 6 October 1875

126 Dato' Maharajalela today is regarded by most Perak Malays as a heroic figure who resisted British imperialism.

127 Pall Mall Gazette 24 February 1876.

128 A 'treaty' port on China's east coast, opposite Korea. Now called Yantai.

129 The Times October 8, 1876

130 E A Reynolds, a local businessman, 1878

131 Alfred wrote one more, final, letter, in June 1868.

132 Hambleden Parish Magazine June 1885.

133 On the present site of the village stores.

134 October 1887

135 October 1878

136 August 1879

137 October 1880

138 December 1880 – note the lateness of the harvest

139 July 1882

140 His estate was valued at £1.75m when he died in 1891 – something over £200m today.

141 February 1879

142 WHS was one of the first to be buried in the new cemetery, at Pheasants Hill, some half a mile from the churchyard.

143 Huddersfield Daily Chronicle.

144 Henry Woodyer was involved in the Anglican high church movement; throughout his career he saw his work as an architect as a means of serving the church.

145 Sadly, no longer there!

146 He had been rector between 1840 and 1882.

147 Now part of Goldsmiths College, part of the University of London.

148 Now a care-home. The magnificent chapel can be seen at https://www.barchester.com/home/st-thomas-care-home

149 Reproduced from *The Royal Navy, China Station: 1864-1941* by Jonathan Parkinson (Matador Press)

150 Later an Admiral and First Sea Lord, often considered the second most important figure in British naval history after Nelson.

151 Thomas Edison has been popularly credited as being the inventor of the incandescent electric lightbulb. While both he and Sir Joseph Wilson Swan were working on either side of the Atlantic to produce a suitable filament for a lightbulb, it was Swan – born in Sunderland – who demonstrated a working incandescent lightbulb using a carbon filament on 3 February 1879 at a meeting of the Literary and Philosophical Society of Newcastle upon Tyne, several months ahead of Edison. It was Swan's bulbs that lit the *Inflexible*.

152 Hampshire Telegraph 5 June 1880

153 Hampshire Telegraph 10 April 1880

154 Hampshire Telegraph 1 May 1880

155 Hampshire Telegraph 19 February 1881.

156 Anna was 75.

157 Sir George was 83; he would die six months later.

158 Times 21 April 1880

159 Letters to Eddy : 16 June 1861

160 Letters to Eddy : 17 July 1861

161 Lord Northbrook, First Lord of the Admiralty, in a letter to Alfred 21 May 1884.

162 New Statesman 10-16 May 2019

163 December 1885

164 Original emphasis

165 December 1885

166 The new church at Skirmett (All Saints) was consecrated on 11 January 1887. It is now a private home.

167 December 1887

168 Western Morning News 2 May 1888

169 12 February 1889

170 They lived at 40/41 Pall Mall, opposite what is now the RAC Club.

171 Quoted by Jan Marsh in Christina Rosetti, a Literary Biography, 1994

172 Select Committee of the House of Lords on the Law Relating to the Protection of Young Girls, 1881

173 A Seaman's life on board a man-of-war : Griffin & Co : Portsmouth : 1881. Published anonymously, but attributed to Admiral Ryder.

174 The age of consent had been set at 12 since 1275! A concern that young girls were being sold into brothels led Parliament to raise the age of consent to 13 in 1875 and to 16 in 1885.

175 He would be drowned on the fateful voyage of the Titanic in 1912.

176 Absorbed into the Evening Standard in 1923.

177 They were repealed in 1886.

178 Prostitution and Victorian Society: Women, Class, and the State : Walkowitz : Cambridge University Press 1982

179 'Tableaux Vivants' were popular, in which female performers often simulated nudity by wearing flesh-coloured body-stockings.

180 A Paper on "purity and the Prevention of the Degradation of Women and Children" by Admiral Ryder, 1885.

181 Now a care home.

182 An historic part of the city of Leicester

183 http://www.edouard-manet.net/le-dejeuner-sur-l-herbe

184 https://www.wikiart.org/en/edouard-manet/olympia-1863

185 https://www.pubhist.com/w6461

186 https://www.tate.org.uk/art/artworks/roussel-the-reading-girl-n04361

187 Spectator, 16 April 1887

188 Is Hunt's '*The Awakening Conscience*' an exception to this? https://www.tate.org.uk/art/artworks/hunt-the-awakening-conscience-t02075

189 On the day before his death in 1896.

190 William Ewart Gladstone recounting the conversation to Lord Rendel in 1889

191 Speech in the House of Commons, 3 March 1831.

192 The Times, 6 February 1885.

193 At the Battle of Omdurman in 1898

194 July 1872

195 The word 'unemployment' entered the Oxford English Dictionary in 1886.

196 In his letter in which he resigned as chairman of the Social Mobility Commission in December 2017, Alan Milburn commented 'The growing sense that we have become an 'us and them' society is deeply corrosive for our cohesion as a nation.' We've come a long way in 130 years!

197 The Life of William Morris : J W Mackail : Longmans, London , 1901

198 Obituary, 16 May 1888

199 The word 'scientist' entered the Oxford English Dictionary in 1840.

200 The Age of Wonder : Richard Holmes : Harper Press, London : 2009

201 On 13 March 1781, Herschel realized that one celestial body he had observed was not a star, but a planet, Uranus. This was the first planet to be discovered since antiquity and Herschel became famous overnight.

202 Deep time is the concept of geologic time.

203 Until Lyell, it was commonly accepted that the creation of the world (Adam and Eve) took place in 4004BC.

204 Hampshire Telegraph 5 May 1888

205 Bradlaugh will be best remembered for having founded the National Secular Society, which he did in 1866, and his pioneering work to make artificial contraception widely available to those of all classes. In 1877 he was tried, with his friend, feminist and socialist, Annie Besant, for publishing a pamphlet supporting birth control. He was sentenced to six months imprisonment and a large fine, but the verdict was overturned on appeal. The churches, however, rigorously opposed artificial contraception. The Church of England abandoned this policy in 1930, but the Roman Catholic Church still retains it.